**W9-DEM-530**

East Smithfield Public Library
50 Esmond Street
Esmond, R.I. 02917
401-231-5150

*Safety,*

*Maintenance,*

*and Operating*

*Instructions*

*for Teens*

# THE GUY BOOK

**AN OWNER'S MANUAL FOR TEENS**

CROWN PUBLISHERS
NEW YORK

*Mavis Jukes*

Copyright © 2002 by Mavis Jukes

Photo credits: page i copyright © Corbis Stock Market. Pages iv, 4, 7, 19, 37, 43, 50, 61, 62, 67, 72, 75, 105, 117, 118, 121, 122, 127, 128, 131, 137: copyright © H. Armstrong Roberts. Pages iii, viii, 20, 28–29, 35, 39, 54, 57, 71, 76, 89, 92, 132, 138: copyright © SuperStock. Pages 10, 22, 30, 44, 58, 81, 85, 95, 107, 114, 144, 147, 148: copyright © Getty Images. Diagrams on pages 12, 32, 36, 146 illustrated by Lisa Paterno-Guinta.

All rights reserved. No part of this book may be reproduced or transmitted in any form or by any means, electronic or mechanical, including photocopying, recording, or by any information storage and retrieval system, without permission in writing from the publisher.

Published by Crown Publishers, a division of Random House, Inc., 1540 Broadway, New York, N.Y. 10036

CROWN and colophon are trademarks of Random House, Inc.

www.randomhouse.com/teens

Book design by Elizabeth Van Itallie

**Library of Congress Cataloging-in-Publication Data**

Jukes, Mavis.

The guy book : an owner's manual : safety, maintenance, and operating instructions for teens / by Mavis Jukes.—1st ed.
p.        cm.
Includes bibliographical references and index.

Summary: Provides information for boys on changes that occur in their bodies during puberty and offers advice on sexual topics, nutrition, drugs, girls, and more.

1. Teenage boys—Juvenile literature. 2. Adolescence—Juvenile literature. 3. Puberty—Juvenile literature. 4. Sex instruction for boys—Juvenile literature. 5. Sex instruction for teenagers—Juvenile literature. 6. Interpersonal relations in adolescence—Juvenile literature. [1. Sex instruction for boys. 2. Puberty. 3. Teenage boys.] I. Title.

HQ797 .J84 2002
305.235—dc21        2001047073

ISBN 0-679-89028-9 (trade pbk.)
ISBN 0-679-99028-3 (lib. bdg.)

Printed in the United States of America

January 2002

10 9 8 7 6 5 4 3 2

*For Bob*

84.148

# Table of CONTENTS

## DISCLAIMER

### *A Note to the Reader*

*The Guy Book: An Owner's Manual* includes information that has been gathered through careful research by the author. Stories have been contributed by guys from a wide range of ages and cultural backgrounds. This book has been reviewed for accuracy by doctors in the areas of pediatrics and adolescent psychology. It has also been reviewed by an attorney. Laws that relate to sex, drugs, alcohol, violence, harassment, paternal responsibilities, and reproductive rights of juveniles vary from state to state. This book isn't a legal reference and shouldn't be used as one. If you have legal questions, talk to an attorney specializing in juvenile law.

Information in the field of sexual health for children and adolescents is continually changing. Every attempt has been made to ensure that this book is scientifically correct, but its purpose is to give general information; it shouldn't be relied on as a source of medical advice. If you have symptoms or specific questions or concerns related to your health, call your doctor. If you have any questions about the material in this book, please consult your parent, guardian, doctor, teacher, school counselor, or other informed, responsible adult.

*Thanks*

—for the editing: Nancy Hinkel
—for the art direction: Isabel Warren-Lynch
—for the book design: Elizabeth Van Itallie
—for review, in the area of adolescent medicine: Dr. Sarah Jane Schwarzenberg
in the area of adolescent psychology: Dr. Alice Siegel
in the area of law: Anke Steinecke
—for the backup: my family, especially my mom, Marguerite Jukes
—for ideas, insight, inspiration, and/or inside information: my friends—
with special thanks to Al, Alan, Bale, Bill, Bill, Bucca, Danny, David,
Dino, Dixon, Eldon, Fred, George, Jaimi, Jim, JoHarvey, Kearn, Lenore, Manuel, Marilyn,
Mary, Mary, Mary Ann, Mike, Milly, Pat, Richard, Richard, Sharon, Simon,
Sonia, Suzanne, Terry, and Wai-Yin

# THE GUY BOOK

When your body begins to change from a kid's body into the body of a young adult, it means you're going through puberty. For most boys, puberty begins at about age 12½ or 13.

But it's also normal for it to begin earlier or later.

Going through puberty includes having your penis and testicles grow bigger. It also includes growing pubic hair and other body hair, sweating more, having oilier skin, growing taller, getting physically stronger, having your voice get lower, producing sperm, ejaculating, and maybe having stronger sexual feelings. All of these things are supposed to happen.

And they're all explained in *The Guy Book*.

*The Guy Book* also contains other information that you may need down the road. It covers a wide range of information, too. Some material may be new to you, some familiar.

It's about sex and sexuality; it explains how sexual intercourse can cause pregnancy and how unplanned pregnancy can be avoided by using birth control.

It also discusses sexually transmitted diseases, including AIDS. It talks about condoms and the correct use of condoms. It deals with other health issues, including alcohol, tobacco, and drug use.

There's some advice included, too—like about how to choose a deodorant and how to shave, tie a tie, dance slow, and put together a wardrobe.

*The Guy Book* isn't meant to take the place of communicating with an actual person—it can't. Talk to your dad, mom, or another trusted adult about concerns or questions you may have that relate to the content of this book.

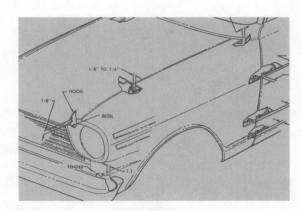

## FEEL READY FOR THE INFORMATION?

If you're not sure, ask your parent or guardian if he or she thinks this book is right for you.

# CHAPTER 1

# *Under the Hood:*
# PARTS

## STANDARD EQUIPMENT

Human reproductive systems include primary reproductive organs, called **gonads**.

A male's gonads are his **testes.** Testes are commonly called "balls." They have dual functions: They produce reproductive cells (**sperm**), and they secrete the sex hormone **testosterone.**

Your reproductive system also includes accessory reproductive organs: a system of ducts that store and carry sperm, and glands that line and empty into these ducts.

The penis has more than one purpose and more than one function. The role of the penis in the reproductive system is to distribute sperm. It's also an organ of excretion: You pee out of it. The penis has another important function: producing intense physical pleasure.

## PARTS

The end of the penis is called the **glans**. It's otherwise known as the "head." It's the most sensitive part to touch.

The glans is covered by a retractable layer of skin called the **foreskin**.

Some boys are **circumcised** at birth—which is when the foreskin is surgically removed. Circumcision is sometimes performed for religious reasons. In terms of appearance, it's considered fine to be circumcised or fine to be left intact.

The glans of an intact penis is reported to be more sensitive than the glans of a circumcised penis.

### FYI Circumcision

Most doctors now agree that there is no medical reason to circumcise every newborn baby boy, and more and more parents in the U.S. are choosing not to do the procedure.

For one thing, routine circumcision of infants is no longer advised for prevention of penis cancer. (*Penis cancer?* Don't worry, young guys very rarely get this.)

Neither is circumcision considered necessary for prevention of infection. Keeping an intact penis clean is easily accomplished by gently pulling back the foreskin and washing under and around it with soap and water. This prevents smegma, the white substance secreted by the glans, from getting trapped behind the foreskin and causing infection.

There are medical reasons for circumcision

in some cases, though. It may be recommended if a guy's foreskin is uncomfortably tight or too big to be moved down over the glans.

Circumcision surgery is relatively simple and straightforward, and it need not be a cause of concern if it becomes necessary. However, it does require surgery for an older child or a man.

The rest of the penis is called the **shaft**. The structure of the penis and the blood flow to and from the tissue inside it (**erectile tissue**) allow the penis to become temporarily rigid at times. This is called having an **erection**. Boys get erections throughout their lives, starting when they are babies. However, erections take on new meaning during puberty (see page 11).

The testes hang down in a pouch of skin called the **scrotum**. One ball is called a **testis**. The scrotum is internally divided into two sacs: one for each testis. The testes-and-scrotum combo is often referred to as **testicles.**

A couple of months before the birth of a male baby, his testes descend into his scrotum. They drop down from his abdomen, where they are formed.

Sometimes a testis doesn't descend. It just stays up in the abdomen or only comes partway down. If you have an undescended testis or partly descended testis, make an appointment to talk to your doctor about it. He or she may recommend correcting this with hormone treatment or surgery.

# OUTSTANDING DESIGN FEATURES
## *Cooling System*

Sperm (more about them on page 11) are manufactured at a lower temperature than the internal temperature of the body. Air circulating around the scrotum keeps the testes cooler. Also, there's a heat-exchange setup in the blood vessels that supply the testes: a cooling system.

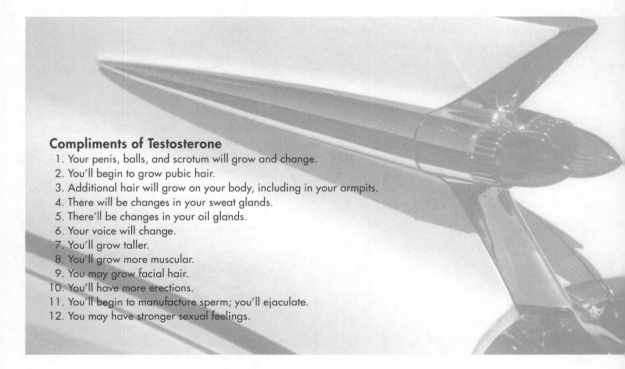

### Compliments of Testosterone
1. Your penis, balls, and scrotum will grow and change.
2. You'll begin to grow pubic hair.
3. Additional hair will grow on your body, including in your armpits.
4. There will be changes in your sweat glands.
5. There'll be changes in your oil glands.
6. Your voice will change.
7. You'll grow taller.
8. You'll grow more muscular.
9. You may grow facial hair.
10. You'll have more erections.
11. You'll begin to manufacture sperm; you'll ejaculate.
12. You may have stronger sexual feelings.

## Heat Regulation

The scrotum is capable of relaxing and tightening up. When it's chilly out, it pulls the testes as close as possible to the body—where they can warm up. When it's hot out, the scrotum gets all soft and droopy so that the testes can kind of swing in the breeze—to cool off.

This design isn't just to keep the testes at the absolute optimum temperature for sperm formation. The testes are unprotected by muscle or bone. This is risky, considering how important they are. To make the best of the situation, the scrotum tightens when a guy feels fear, drawing his testes closer to his body, where they will be safer if there is a confrontation.

It can also tighten when a guy feels nervous, and it tightens during sex.

One testis is usually a little bit bigger than the other. Both are carefully located in the scrotum so that one hangs lower than the other, usually the left one. This way, they aren't in a position to crush each other as a guy goes about an active daily life—that involves running, for instance.

# CONTROL PANELS
## Hormones

Hormones are part of a communication system called the **endocrine system**. They are chemicals secreted by various organs of the body, including the brain, heart, kidneys, liver, thyroid gland, and testes. Hormones act like tiny messengers, circulating through the bloodstream and giving signals to cells to make changes that affect everything from brain development to kidney function.

Even though hormones are carried by the blood throughout the entire body and reach all the body's tissues, hormones are very specific as to which cells they influence. Sex hormones are present in both males and females, and reproductive functions are largely controlled by them. Males and females share some of the same sex hormones.

The main male sex hormone is testosterone. It's secreted in the testes by **Leydig cells**, which are located in connective-tissue spaces between the tubules where sperm are formed.

Testosterone is famous for contributing to a boy's attraction to action. It enables guys to have the energy and concentration to perform well in a variety of situations.

Testosterone triggers many of the changes associated with puberty. It tells a guy's reproductive (sex) organs how and when to develop.

**Secondary sexual characteristics** aren't directly involved in reproduction, but they make up the many differences between male and female bodies.

Testosterone influences the development of these characteristics. Among other things, it deepens the voice, increases lean muscle mass, cuts down on body fat, increases bone density and growth, and triggers the growth of facial hair.

It also increases sex drive (**libido**).

# CHAPTER 2

# IGNITION
## *System:* HOW IT ALL WORKS

## YOUR PENIS AND TESTICLES WILL GROW AND CHANGE

### *What to Expect*

When puberty begins, the following changes take place over the course of a few years:

A very small amount of straight, almost colorless hair grows at the base of the penis; the penis becomes slightly enlarged; the scrotum becomes larger and less smooth than it used to be. On lighter-skinned boys, the scrotum will look pink. The coloring on darker-skinned guys will deepen.

The scrotum will get longer and looser and will hang lower. The testes will begin to grow. Oil and sweat glands will begin to develop on the skin of the penis and scrotum.

The hair at the base of the penis (pubic hair) gradually becomes darker (these hairs may be preceded by little bumps); the hair will begin to curl; the penis becomes longer and wider; the scrotum and testes will continue to grow. One testis will hang lower than the other.

The amount of pubic hair increases, and it becomes coarse.

The penis becomes larger (thicker), and the scro-

tum continues to grow; the skin on the penis and scrotum becomes visibly darker.

Pubic hair fills in. It can be red, brown, black, or blond. It can be very, *very* curly, or it can be almost straight. It makes a triangular shape (upside down) that spreads to the inner thighs (this is the adult pattern) and around the anus; the penis and scrotum reach adult size.

### HEADS UP! Hood Ornaments

If you're thinking of piercing your penis, here are a few things to consider:

Piercing equipment needs to be sterile in order to prevent the transfer of germs—including those that cause AIDS and hepatitis. Piercing should only be done by a professional.

Body piercings don't always heal completely, and any unhealed wound, no matter how small, can provide an entry point for germs.

### *You'll grow armpit hair and you'll get furrier.*

During puberty, boys grow hair in the armpits. Boys may also grow hair on the chest, back, and shoulders. Hair on the legs will thicken.

A line of fuzzy hair, sometimes referred to as a

## PENIS SPECIFICATIONS

The average adult penis size is approximately $3\frac{1}{2}$ to $4\frac{1}{2}$ inches long. Shorter or longer is also normal. The average length of an erect penis is about 6 inches. Erect penises are pretty much the same size.

### ✔ Penis Size

Since penises are so noticeable, it's natural for boys to compare.
   During puberty, there is quite a range of sizes. That's because boys go through puberty at different rates; some begin the process earlier than others.

### ✔ A Few Things to Keep in Mind

1. The notion that a large penis is an indication of great masculinity (or great sexual ability) is a myth.
2. All size penises work.
3. A relatively small penis will get significantly bigger when it becomes erect.
4. Science has never shown any correlation between ethnic background and penis size.
5. Penises look different from different angles; looking down at one from above makes it seem shorter than it actually is.
6. The size of a penis is not a measure of how often a boy will get an erection, how often he will ejaculate, or how his orgasms will feel.
7. Penis size doesn't relate to the ability a boy will have to please his sexual partner when he grows up. Pleasing a sexual partner has much more to do with communicating with, caring about, understanding the sexual responses of, and respecting the other person.
8. People don't generally choose partners based on what size penis a guy has.

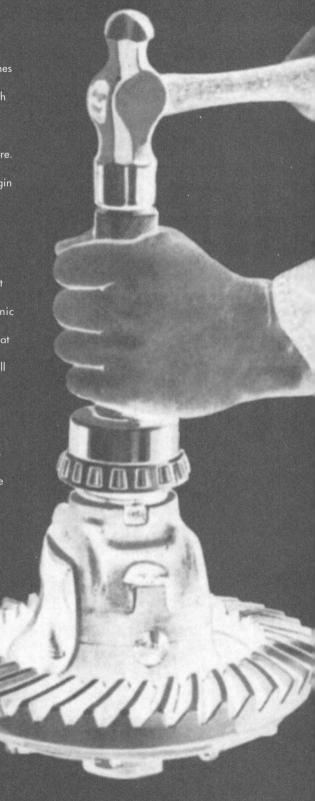

"happy trail," may grow between a guy's belly button and his pubic area.

## *New sweat glands will begin to work. You'll sweat more. You'll smell stronger.*

Puberty causes sweat glands to work overtime; you'll sweat more. Your armpits and genital area will have an odor that's different from when you were a little kid.

Wearing deodorant is helpful when it comes to armpit odor and perspiration control—but not all people feel a need to use it. Citations aren't issued for sweating. If you wash regularly and wear clean clothes, you'll smell fine—even if you happen to work up a sweat. But wash your clothes often. T-shirts, socks, and underwear, since they're worn very close to the body, get ripe fast once you've reached puberty.

## OIL CHANGES
*Your skin will become oilier. You may develop pimples on your face, shoulders, and back.*

At puberty, oil glands start to produce an oily substance called **sebum**. Sebum is emptied onto the surface of the skin out of tiny openings called **pores**.

### *Bumps Ahead*

During puberty, oil glands can get revved up by hormones and produce too much sebum.

Sebum can end up filling the duct, clogging the pore, and forming a blackhead. (Blackheads are not dirty pores. The black part of a blackhead is just sebum, which darkens when it comes in contact with the air.)

Sebum can build up and rupture the wall of the oil gland and escape into the surrounding skin tissue, causing inflammation and **pus** (a pimple).

## GUY REPORT: THE LONELY ARMPIT

"Moving from grade school to junior high school, from the sixth grade to the seventh grade, from twelve to thirteen, was one of the most traumatic periods of my life. For the first time, I had to go to gym class and be in the shower naked with other boys! And all of them, it seemed, were fully developed 'hairy men.' They had it all over them . . . on their chests, their faces, under their arms. And most dadlike and manly of all—they had pubic hair!

"To my horrid chagrin, I only had hair growing in my left armpit . . . no hair anywhere else! It was terrifying and humiliating, and I spent the entire year trying to hide my freakish body—front to the bricks, right arm down, and left arm up. (I had to show something!) Finally, by the eighth grade, to my great relief, some fuzz started showing up."

### *Acne*

Acne is the result of having many plugged-up oil glands. Some forms of acne require continuous, consistent treatment by a physician over a period of months or years. The good news is that acne can be successfully managed and almost everybody outgrows it, eventually.

A **dermatologist** (skin specialist) can develop a treatment plan for acne. The plan may involve applying medicated cream or gel directly onto the skin, washing the skin with medicated washes, and/or taking prescription medications orally (by mouth).

Make and keep appointments as advised.

Under some circumstances, blood tests may be required at intervals to make sure that your body is tolerating the medications safely.

### *Your voice will change.*

At about age 14 or 15, your voice will change to a lower, adult tone. This is because the voice box gets larger during puberty and your vocal cords, inside the voice box, get longer.

Lowering of the voice usually doesn't present a problem, except for an occasional embarrassing squeak. Some boys try to control this by speaking in a calm and controlled manner.

Try not to worry about this temporary situation; the people around you, girls included, kind of expect this to happen—given that a voice change at puberty is a normal experience for every guy who walks the earth!

Eventually your voice will settle into its adult range, and the sudden shifts won't happen anymore.

### *You'll grow taller.*

Once a guy's sex organs have begun to develop, he will experience a growth spurt of about 3½ inches a year (remember: this is average growth; more or less can still be normal). Fast growth usually continues for about 3 years, then slows down, stopping at about age 20.

Even though girls and boys begin to go through puberty at approximately the same time, the growth spurt for girls begins at an earlier stage of puberty than it does for boys (see page 65).

**FYI  Your Bones**
If your feet seem big in comparison to the rest of your body, it's because . . . well, they are!
Not all bones of the body grow at the same rate during the growth spurt. Bones in the arms, legs, and (especially) the feet get a jump

on some of the rest of the bones of the body.

For a while, it might seem as if your shoe size is going to get (or has already gotten) completely out of hand. If you're worried about this, there's good news. Your feet will stop growing bigger before you will stop growing taller.

So it all works out in the end.

### *You'll become physically stronger.*

Your shoulders will become broader and more muscular, and muscles will grow bigger in your thighs, calves, and upper arms.

So you'll become physically stronger than you were when you were a little kid. How much bigger and stronger?

It's impossible to know what your body shape and size will ultimately be.

## ACCEPT YOUR BODY TYPE

Sure, we admire and appreciate the bodies of professional athletes and Olympians. But we all aren't genetically programmed to develop the physique of an outstanding athlete or to attain the idealized male body images portrayed in the media. Try to maintain realistic expectations for yourself and the others around you.

A reasonable goal? Be fit. It's not a requirement to be athletic, but be active.

Live an active lifestyle and eat well. Build some form of exercise into your routine daily life. When you're growing, it's extra important for your body to get all the nutrients it needs. Eat for energy, eat to satisfy hunger, eat for enjoyment—and eat for nutrition. And eat on time! Being hungry can make it hard to concentrate or cause you to feel grumpy or down in the dumps and unmotivated (see page 31).

## You may grow whiskers.

Most boys begin to grow facial hair between the ages of 14 and 18. Some guys just do not grow whiskers—not a mustache, beard, goatee, or sideburns. How much facial hair you have is genetically determined.

If you want to know how hairy your face will be, you may get some clues from checking out the other (adult) males in your family.

How little or much facial hair a guy can grow isn't a measure of masculinity.

### FYI Breast Changes

Breast changes happen to boys as well as girls during puberty. Boys' nipples grow slightly bigger and get darker. The area around the nipple (areola) gets wider and darker.

Your breasts may ache as you go through puberty, and you may have some temporary breast growth. Don't worry! Temporary breast growth is so normal it even has a name: gynecomastia.

Gynecomastia disappears, usually before most people even learn the name of it, within about a year.

Questions? Ask your doctor.

## You may have more erections.

Erections happen either spontaneously or when a guy becomes sexually excited.

Spontaneous erections happen on their own, without any physical encouragement. Guys often wake up with an erection.

An erect penis sticks out and stands up, away from the body. It becomes longer, thicker, and harder. It may bend to one side or the other.

Touching the penis, especially the head of the penis, can stimulate this reaction.

But so can certain thoughts, fantasies, emotions, sights, and smells.

## Spontaneous Erections

Spontaneous erections are the result of a guy's fluc-tuating or high levels of testosterone. They slowly go away on their own if the penis is ignored.

## Down, boy!

It's totally normal for a boy's penis to spring up several times a day and sometimes for no apparent reason—or for a very apparent reason. Like seeing somebody sexy!

It's also totally normal for this not to happen! There's no rule that says a teenage boy has to have continual erections at the drop of a hat.

A penis may simply react to the presence of naked bodies, regardless of gender. So if you get (or somebody else gets) an erection in the locker room, just ignore it. A penis is a very complex, excitable organ, and guys can't always get it to cooperate or be cool. Sometimes it just has its own deal going. If it goofs around in the locker room, don't let it stress you.

### ➤ Face it.

You wouldn't trade it in.

Your penis may get bigger (or smaller) at what seems to be exactly the wrong moment.

It will forever be capable of producing a certain amount of stress or embarrassment, and it might not be 100 percent dependable (including during sex). But it will be pretty much reliable. And definitely worth having!

The good news is that it will at least become more predictable as you get older.

## You'll begin to manufacture sperm.

Sperm begins to be manufactured about a year or so after the penis, testes, and scrotum begin to grow—at about the time that your pubic hair is filling in.

Sperm contain half of the genetic information needed to create a baby. Once a boy starts producing sperm, it means that he has become physically capable of fathering a child (see page 73). A mature male produces about 30 million sperm every day, and the production of sperm happens round the clock—24-7.

## SPERM

The head of a sperm contains DNA—which is the substance bearing the sperm's genetic information. The info is contained in 23 **chromosomes**.

The midpiece of the sperm provides energy for the sperm's movement, which is accomplished by a tail.

The tail is made up of filaments that produce whiplike movements. These movements propel the sperm forward—in search of a female reproductive cell (**ovum**).

Should the 23 chromosomes in a sperm be united with the twenty-three chromosomes contained in a female reproductive cell (ovum), the combined 46 chromosomes will provide the complete set of plans needed to make a new human being.

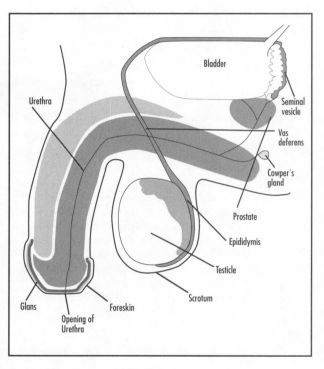

Bladder

Urethra

Seminal vesicle

Vas deferens

Cowper's gland

Prostate

Epididymis

Testicle

Scrotum

Glans

Opening of Urethra

Foreskin

The duct of the **epididymis** drains each testis into a large, thick-walled tube called a **vas deferens**. The two vas deferens tubes and the part of the duct of the epididymis closest to the vas deferens tubes serve as storage reservoirs for sperm.

The vas deferens tubes are bound together in the **spermatic cord**, which passes through a small passage into the abdomen. Once inside the abdomen, they become the **ejaculatory ducts**.

Two large glands called the **seminal vesicles** feed into the vas deferens just before this transitional point. The ejaculatory ducts pass through the **prostate gland**, a single doughnut-shaped gland.

Seminal vesicles and the prostate gland secrete a milky-whitish fluid, which bathes, energizes, and nourishes sperm. The milky fluid, with millions of frisky sperm suspended in it, is called **semen**.

The ejaculatory ducts join up with the **urethra**, a tube that comes from the bladder and runs through the penis, all the way out to the tip.

The urethra has two jobs: one is to carry pee out of the body, and the other is to carry semen out of the body. Before semen is carried out, a valve automatically closes off the bladder so that peeing becomes impossible during this process.

## *Coils and Distributor*

**Spermatogenesis** (sperm production) begins in tiny, tightly coiled **tubules** (tiny tubes) located inside your testes. This is how it starts:

Triggered by testosterone, original sperm cells (**spermatogonia**) begin to divide—initiating a cycle of cell division, which will continue throughout a male's life. The process of cell division results in the cloning (re-creating) of original cells so that

the supply never runs out. But different cell forms are also created in the process. These different cells morph through a series of complex changes and are ultimately remodeled into sperm: cells that have heads, midpieces, and tails.

As sperm form, they are moved through the tubules into a system of ducts, ending up in a single duct inside of a structure called the **epididymis**. The epididymis is loosely attached to the outside of the

**GUY REPORT: ON WET DREAMS**

"The first time it happened to me, I thought I wet the bed.

"It woke me up enough for me to figure out that the wet spot was only on a very small area of the sheet. And there was sticky fluid on my inner thigh.

"The next morning the sheet had a yellowish stain on it. My thigh had a film on it that looked like dried-up paste.

"I didn't know what it was, and I was too embarrassed to ask. . . ."

testis. Sperm continue to mature while traveling through the epididymis, a trip that takes about 12 days. The complete cycle of a sperm developing and maturing takes about 64 days.

## *You'll ejaculate.*

As soon as you ejaculate for the first time, you will know that sperm production has begun. Ejaculation (commonly called "coming") is when semen is discharged from your penis. Ejaculation can happen while you're awake or asleep.

Having an ejaculation is a landmark event, similar to when a girl starts her period (see page 66). But even though ejaculating means you've become physically mature, it doesn't mean you've become a man—any more than it means that a girl has become a woman just because she's started menstruating.

Everybody remains a kid for quite a while after reaching puberty, and so will you. You'll still be a kid, entitled to the love, care, and protection of the adults around you. You won't (and shouldn't) be expected to take on adult roles and responsibilities.

Ejaculating while sleeping is called having a nocturnal emission, or a wet dream. Having a wet dream is a way of releasing sperm that builds up inside of your body.

Most guys have wet dreams, but some guys don't. Guys who release a lot of sperm by masturbating (see page 15) don't usually have as many wet dreams.

Wet dreams can be accompanied by a feeling of intense pleasure (an orgasm), but often they're not. Ejaculation while sleeping can be a completely non-sensual event; it can just involve waking up with a wet spot on your sheets, pajamas, and/or underwear.

## *No Problem*

Wet dreams are normal and should be expected. If you have a wet dream—good. Go back to sleep.

Sheets dry on their own just fine. It's not necessary to rip your whole bed apart and wash your

**GUY REPORT: THE OPEN ROAD**

"My dad had a 1950 red Chevy pickup. When he drove down the dirt roads through the ranch, I used to ride in the back. (Now it's against the law; it wasn't then.)

"One day I had a revelation. I had thrown my body over the side of the pickup bed, riding it Indian-style—like some Comanche lying on one side of his horse while someone was shooting at him from the other side. The motion of the truck became very pleasing. My Levis were jiggling right along with the metal. I suddenly had my first (significantly remembered) orgasm. I was thrilled and stunned.

"I remember sitting in the bed of the truck afterward, wondering why this feeling made me want to be around girls forever. I had NEVER wanted to be around girls before!

"In retrospect, I think this is pretty funny, but at the time it was overwhelmingly mysterious and even spooky. My first sexual experience—involved a truck!

"No wonder I grew up to love moving vehicles and the open road."

sheets every time some semen gets on them, so don't.

If you do your own wash, note that washing semen spots out of light-colored fabric in very hot water can cause stains. Warm water is better.

## Ejaculating While Awake

Some boys ejaculate for the first time while awake—kind of accidentally. And it surprises them.

## How It All Happens

Before and during ejaculation, a nerve center at the base of the spine starts calling the signals, and nerve impulses occur, setting off a chain of reactions:

Blood vessels in the penis **dilate** (widen). Blood rushes in and fills the erectile tissue at high pressure. The penis becomes longer, thicker, and harder. Engorged with blood, the tissue expands, compressing the vessels that drain it. This helps keep the tissue rigid and the penis erect. Skin color darkens and the scrotum tightens.

The smooth muscles of the ducts and glands contract, emptying sperm and glandular secretions into the urethra. Semen is expelled from the urethra by a series of contractions of the smooth muscle that surrounds it—and also by contractions of the muscle at the base of the penis.

These contractions are associated with intense sensations of pleasure—called **having an orgasm**. Leading up to and during an orgasm, the heart rate increases noticeably, and breathing becomes faster than normal.

## During an ejaculation . . .

About a teaspoonful of semen comes out. It comes out during a series of about four or five spurts that happen one right after another.

The semen can shoot out for quite a distance (a couple of feet), spurt out (a couple of inches), or even just dribble or leak out; the texture of the

semen can also vary. Sometimes it's thick; other times it's thin. It smells kind of sweet.

The experience of ejaculating and having an orgasm is completely variable. It can be more or less intense, depending on the occasion. Sometimes having an orgasm is nothing short of an earth-shattering event; other times it's just a quick, mildly pleasant feeling.

The amount of semen involved can also vary; the quantity can depend on how much time has passed since the last ejaculation. The more time between ejaculations, the more semen.

While it's possible to ejaculate without having an orgasm and possible to have an orgasm without ejaculating, these two events usually happen at the same time.

However, life is full of surprises. Boys are capable of having an orgasm without ejaculating—when experiencing something very sensual and exciting.

### HEADS UP!

Before ejaculation occurs, a drop of clear fluid will appear at the tip of your penis. This is called "pre-ejaculate." Pre-ejaculate clears the way for semen: It neutralizes the pathway of the urethra in case there are traces of urine, which can impair sperm.

It is important to know that there is usually some live sperm in this fluid. It's not likely, but it is possible, for pre-ejaculate to cause pregnancy (see page 94).

The pre-ejaculate of an infected person can also contain germs, including HIV—the virus that causes AIDS (see page 87).

## "Blue Balls"

If you remain sexually excited for a very long period of time without ejaculating, you may experience discomfort in your testicles (achy balls).

The discomfort has a nickname: "blue balls." Happily, your balls will not turn blue. The aching can be relieved by masturbating or by just wait-

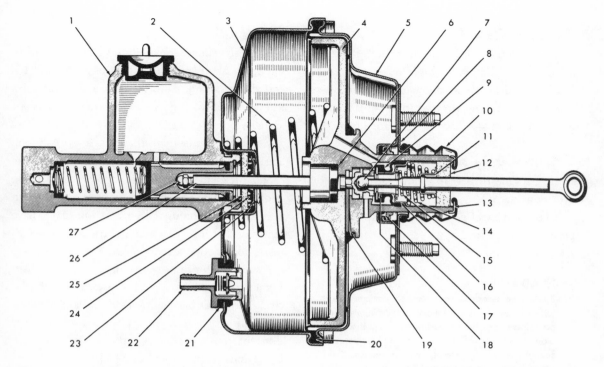

1  2  3  4  5  6  7  8  9  10  11  12  13  14  15  16  17  18  19  20  21  22  23  24  25  26  27

ing. The pain goes away by itself after a while.

Blue balls should not be used as an excuse for a guy to try to pressure his partner to have sex with him.

## *Masturbating (or "Solo Sex")*

Some boys ejaculate for the first time by **masturbating.**

The purpose of masturbation is to give comfort. Masturbating can also relieve tension.

A guy masturbates by touching, rubbing, pressing, and/or stroking his penis (and maybe his balls). If he keeps on doing this, he will usually become sexually aroused, ejaculate, and have an orgasm.

Almost all boys who have reached puberty masturbate; many masturbate daily, some several times a day.

How often is too often? There's no easy answer to this question.

But becoming obsessed by masturbation or feeling compelled to masturbate over and over again as a means of escape are reasons for discussing masturbation with your doctor or other health care professional (see pages 27, 45).

Masturbation is rumored to cause problems with eyesight and athletic ability, but no way is this true. It doesn't cause hairy palms. Neither does it use up all of a guy's sperm. Sperm is made continuously, so the supply is endless. (However, it's usually necessary for some amount of time to pass between ejaculations.)

For boys who feel okay about it, masturbating is a perfectly safe form of sexual exploration—not at all harmful. It's a healthy, normal, natural expression of sexuality.

While it is perfectly natural and healthy to masturbate, it's also perfectly healthy and normal *not* to. Not all boys want to; not all guys feel good about it. Some religions prohibit it.

If it stresses you out, don't do it. There's certainly no obligation to masturbate.

## Thar she blows!

Whatever you do, don't cap the opening of the tip of your penis with your finger when ejaculating!

This can drive the semen backward, and it can even end up in the wrong tanks — bladder and prostate gland — where it can cause problems.

## Masturbating with Friends

Some guys masturbate in groups; others wouldn't even consider it.

If you don't feel good about group masturbation, don't do it. If you feel it's wrong, it *is* wrong — for you.

**HEADS UP!**
If someone outside of your own, similar age group (either older or younger) is present, definitely don't participate in group masturbation. A significantly older person shouldn't in any way be involved sexually with a significantly younger person. Child abuse is the issue (see page 120).

## Inflation Issues

Sometimes, for no apparent reason (even when a guy is sexually aroused and ready to roll), there will be an unwelcome surprise: Your penis will just go limp.

As previously noted, the penis is not always cooperative, not completely predictable, and not consistently reliable. Loss of erection, or not even getting an erection in the first place, is an event that most males experience on occasion.

If it happens to you, don't panic. Understand that this is normal. Don't get down on yourself about it, and don't make doomsday predictions about your sexual ability. You're fine.

Try again later.

**FYI  Penis Check**
When a guy's penis becomes consistently unreliable, it's advisable to see a doctor. There can be a number of causes for this treatable condition; stress can be a factor. Not knowing what's up and worrying about it adds to stress. He needs to get checked so he can get back on track!

## Fantasies

You might spend considerable time imagining having sexual experiences. Lots of people do! It's called **fantasizing**. Fantasizing is a safe way for a kid to imagine being in a sexual situation without actually being in one.

Fantasizing while masturbating is a very common activity. And fantasizing can get pretty creative.

Same-sex fantasies are especially common during adolescence, when feelings about friendship can become a little confused, so it's not unusual to have fantasies that involve a best guy friend. These fantasies don't define sexual orientation (see page 80).

It's normal for some boys to fantasize about having a sexual encounter with a sister or other relative; many kids have fantasies about family members during their teen years. These fantasies are very different from actual incest within the family, which is a serious problem (see page 134).

If any of your fantasies disturb you, dream up something else to fantasize about or just stop fantasizing for a while. It's not like you *have to* fantasize!

## Hazard Light

If you're seriously thinking about actually *acting on* an unlawful or inappropriate fantasy, don't. Talk to a counselor. Your doctor can refer you. A counselor can help you identify what might be causing you to contemplate doing something regrettable or harmful to someone else or yourself.

**HEADS UP!**
Flashing (exhibitionism) is never okay.
It is wrong and against the law for a guy to intentionally expose his genitals (or butt) for the purpose of shocking or getting a reaction from an unsuspecting person or persons.

A guy can get arrested for doing this, and if convicted, in addition to whatever other penalties a judge may impose, he may be required to identify himself as a sex offender wherever he goes.

Likewise, masturbating in public or in a

situation where you're "accidentally on purpose" likely to get caught by an unsuspecting person is a form of exhibitionism. It's taken very seriously; it can have the same consequences as flashing, if not worse ones.

## Looking at Sexy Pictures

Looking at regular old garden-variety sexy pictures, like mail-order lingerie catalogs or posters of supermodels, isn't exactly unpredictable behavior for teen boys and it's not exactly a crime! Don't guilt yourself out about it. But stay away from pornography (porn).

## Pornography

**Pornography** includes X-rated videos, films, photos, or other images depicting explicit sexual material. It's commonly called "porn." If an adult offers to show you porn, consider it a sexual advance. Decline the offer, and report it to another adult. Showing kids porn is a tactic commonly used by molesters (see page 126).

Don't let curiosity get the best of you. You may be curious, but Internet porn sites are not good places for kids to learn about sex. Think about it: Why have a bunch of potentially weird sexual images floating around in your head before you've even figured out what's going on with your own sexuality?

## You may have stronger sexual feelings.

During puberty, people commonly discover that they have increased sexual feelings. It doesn't mean there's something wrong with you if you don't. Not all guys do.

## Romantic Attractions

Puberty is famous for being a time when people can have pretty strong physical reactions (attractions) to each other (see page 78). But not everybody experiences these.

## Attractions to Adults

You may find yourself sexually attracted to adult movie stars, models, and other adult celebs.

You may also develop crushes on adults you know, such as your teachers, coaches, your friends' parents, etc.

These temporary attractions are a normal part of growing up. As long as they're not acted on, they're fine.

## Hazard Light

Adults know that preadolescents and teens are prone to crushes on adults.

They also know it's totally wrong and against the law for an adult to respond sexually to a kid under the age of consent. If an adult you have a crush on wants to return your affection physically, the adult is out of line. Don't enter into the relationship. Tell another adult what's going on (see page 129)!

## Attractions to Relatives

You might be surprised by sexual feelings toward your relatives of either sex. Getting a crush on a relative is very common. While it's perfectly natural for a kid to feel attracted to a family member, it's not okay to act on those feelings in a sexual way.

## Hazard Light

Occasionally, an adult (or significantly older or more powerful kid) relative may try to get sexual with a kid (or kids) in the family. If this happens to you, refuse. Do *not* blame yourself. Tell another adult what happened and/or call the Child Help USA National Child Abuse Hot Line (see page 46). The hot line is for teens (and adults), too.

# CHAPTER 3

# EXTERIOR
## *Maintenance:*
### BASIC CARE

## UNDERBODY MAINTENANCE

### *Caring for Your Genitals*

Wash them every day or two with soap and water.

### *Detailing*

If you're not circumcised, pay special attention to cleaning under your foreskin.

### *Self-Exam*

About once a month, it's a good idea to examine your testicles. Why? Even though cancer is very, *very* rare among teens, testicular cancer does occur in young men. It begins in the cells that manufacture sperm. It grows into a lump that can be felt.

Testicular cancer can be cured if detected and treated early.

After taking a shower or bath, feel each testicle separately. Using the fingers and thumbs of both hands, gently roll each testicle around (fingers under the testicle, thumbs on top).

Note the epididymis, a structure that is loosely attached to the outside of each testis (on the back). It belongs there (see page 12).

If you discover a small lump, don't panic. Most lumps are cysts (lumps filled with fluid), not cancer. But do have all lumps checked by a doctor just to make sure!

### *Protect Your Genitals from Injury*

A jockstrap (athletic supporter) hugs the genitals close to the body, supporting them and making them less vulnerable to injury during sports. A cup, which fits into the front of a jockstrap, affords extra protection.

Jockstraps are sold in stores that sell athletic equipment—uniforms and that kind of stuff.

They are also sold in department stores, usually the men's and boys' underwear department.

## PREVENTING SURFACE DETERIORATION

### *"Jock Rot"*

What an insulting name for a common condition: having a damp feeling and sore, red, itchy skin around your testicles and on your inner thighs.

Happily, when a guy has jock rot, nothing is rotting.

# FIX-IT TICKETS

In terms of genital care, the following situations absolutely require a pit stop. Go to the doctor and get checked out if you . . .

- ☐ Have pain in your genitals or lower abdomen
- ☐ Have an injury to your testicles
- ☐ Develop a sore or tender spot on your testicles, groin, or genital area
- ☐ Notice a lump on a testicle, in the groin, or in the genital area
- ☐ Have a discharge (pus) come out of the tip of your penis
- ☐ Develop a yellowy-white discharge that's odorless
- ☐ Have a milky discharge (not semen)
- ☐ Have milky urine
- ☐ Have a burning sensation while peeing or have pain in your urethra
- ☐ Have an urgent and/or frequent need to pee
- ☐ Have a foul odor under your foreskin
- ☐ Have warts growing on or around your genitals
- ☐ Have itching, burning, redness, rash, or raised bumps in your genital area
- ☐ Have a painless, clearly visible ulcer on your penis
- ☐ Have painful sores or blisters on your genitals, butt, or thighs
- ☐ Have any other bothersome or painful symptom or condition that worries you

The way to avoid jock rot (or "jock itch") is to wear clean and dry clothing (cotton underwear); also, don't wear pants that are irritating to your crotch.

A little cornstarch is rumored to take care of jock itch in some cases, but it might require a **fungicide**—which kills fungus, the underlying cause of the problem. Fungicides are sold in the drugstore; just ask the pharmacist for a recommendation.

If the condition doesn't improve, be sure to contact your doctor. The rash may have a cause that requires medical attention.

## HEADS UP!
If you have *extreme* pain in your testicles (perhaps following hard physical exertion), get medical attention immediately. Rarely, testicles become twisted. This is a medical emergency.

## WASHING THE SURFACE
*Many guys shower every day.*

Be considerate of the environment; be aware of the amount of water you use and the energy it takes to heat it.

In other words: Shower and get outta there!

Reuse your towel. If you arrange it nicely someplace to dry (like on the towel rack?), it will be more appealing to use again.

And of course, it always helps not to drop, step on, and stand on your towel between uses.

Not every guy has the opportunity to shower daily.

If your living situation doesn't allow for you to, no problem. All anybody needs is soap, water, and a sink or washbasin.

Wash and rinse your face, neck, behind your ears, armpits, genitals, and rear with water, soap, and a washcloth. In that order: face first and rear last.

Also: Brush your teeth, morning and night.

### *Keep Your Face Clean*
To help avoid pimples, blackheads, and whiteheads, wash your face twice a day with warm water and mild soap. What's a mild soap? Ask your pharmacist. Pharmacists can be some

## GUY REPORT: JOCKSTRAPS
Guy #1: "When I was in the sixth grade, my family stayed with relatives in San Antonio, Texas. We temporarily stayed with my aunt and uncle—who sold graves to people before they were dead.

"I went to a huge school, and I had to change classes all day like in a high school. This was new to me. I had to take the city buses to get to the school; also, I had to look after my little brother. In gym class one day, the coach said, 'Okay. I want everybody next week to have your gym clothes—tennis shoes, shorts, T-shirt, and jockstrap.'

"Whoa!

"I was glad the stay in San Antonio was only temporary. I hoped we could hurry up and move so I wouldn't have to bring up jockstraps to my parents. I dreaded telling them I needed a jockstrap. Especially because I had no idea why I did need one! I didn't want to appear ignorant.

"Despite repeated warnings from my coach, I was able to hold out until we moved; I never had the conversation with my parents.

"My next school was also in Texas. The kids didn't even wear shoes much in that school and rejected shoes while playing sports; they felt shoes 'slowed 'em down.'

"There were lots of jocks there—just no straps."

Guy #2: "All I remember about my first jockstrap is the sense of relief I felt when I realized that the 'size: small' referred to the waistband."

of the most helpful people on the planet.

If you are prone to pimples, avoid using perfumed or deodorant soaps, which can make matters worse.

There are over-the-counter cleansers and medicated soaps specifically designed for attacking zits, but don't overdo them. Overusing these products actually can make pimples worse instead of better.

Remember, a mild soap and warm water twice a day is probably all you need to keep your skin clean.

## Spot Removal

It's tempting to try to pop and squeeze pimples and blackheads, but don't. Squeezing, rubbing, pressure, and friction all aggravate acne. Popping and picking can cause scarring.

If you have a habit of rubbing your face or sitting with your chin cupped in your hand, don't. Try to keep your hands off your face. Don't fiddle with bumps or scabs.

Avoid using oily hair and skin products. Check the labels of the products you buy. Many hair and skin care products are oil-free and those are preferable if you have acne.

Ingrown hairs causing zits? See page 9.

Unless you have identified or strongly suspect a

specific food allergy, don't stress too much about snacks. Snack foods—including chocolate and chips—do not cause acne. In moderation, snack foods are fine. But do eat well. There are plenty of options for healthy snacks. Eating well contributes to good health in general—including the health of the skin (see page 31).

(see page 31)

### HEADS UP!
Acne out of control?
Bummed about it?
Talk to your doctor. You may need to be on a supervised, long-term skin care program to get the results you want.

## *Lotion and Sunblock*

Whatever the shade of your skin, it's the right shade. Nobody's skin is too dark or too light.

A little lotion (oil-free is available) will make dry skin feel soft and smooth. And lotion will bring out the deep, rich tones of darker skin.

The lighter the skin and the lighter your eyes, the higher your risk for developing skin cancer from exposure to ultraviolet rays of the sun. But anybody can get skin cancer. Wear sunblock (oil-free is available) and a hat (if practical) when you plan to be outside for extended periods—playing or watching outdoor sports, hiking, climbing, skateboarding, snowboarding, skiing, swimming, surfing, sailing, etc.

Unprotected exposure to the sun can cause damaging sunburns, which may contribute to developing melanoma (cancer of the melanocyte) and premature aging of the skin later on in life.

Stay out of tanning salons.

Tans fade, but unhealthy effects of exposure to ultraviolet rays linger on.

## TRIM
### *Guy Advice: Instructions for Using an Electric Shaver*

1. Plug the shaver in (keep it away from water, so you don't get shocked to death) and turn it on. If it's a rechargeable battery-operated razor, you won't have to plug it in—just take it off the charger and turn it on.

2. Rub it around your face. Use light pressure.

3. You may have to make some faces at yourself in the mirror to get to the hard-to-reach places, like under your nose.

4. When you're done, flip it open and brush the whiskers out. Or blow 'em out. Over the trash can or sink, of course.

5. If it's battery-operated, return the razor to the charger—which plugs into the wall socket.

6. If you want to, you can sprinkle a little aftershave (astringent) lotion into one palm, rub your palms together, and rub it on your face. It feels good.

7. If you use aftershave, don't get carried away with it.

### FUZZ-FACE: GUY REPORT ON SHAVING

"When I was old enough to stand at the bathroom sink and watch my father shave, it was still an art form. Shaving mug, brush, straight razor, and hot towels. Pulling the nose up to get under there. Pursing the lips and wonking them left or right. Lifting the chin to get at the neck. Finishing off the job with some smelly stuff.

"Later, shaving became a craft—still a ritual, but faster, and the tools less beautiful.

"Then came the electric shaver.

"What a disappointment.

"I had watched my father shave for many years so that I'd know what to do—with mug, brush, razor, and towels.

"What started out seeming like a grand adventure ended up being just like mowing the lawn."

## GUY REPORT: INSTRUCTIONS FOR SHAVING WITH A SAFETY RAZOR

"Here's how I shave with a safety razor:

"I use a double-bladed cartridge and shaving cream for sensitive skin. (But you'll have to figure out which products work best for you.)

"I rinse my face with warm water.

"I dispense some shaving cream from the aerosol can onto the fingertips of one hand and apply the cream to the areas to be shaved: above upper lip, below lower lip, chin, sideburns, cheeks, neck.

"I usually start above my upper lip. I stick my tongue up between my top front teeth and my upper lip to make the area firm for shaving.

"I press lightly on my skin and drag the razor downward in short strokes.

"I do the same thing for the area under my lower lip, above my chin. (I put my tongue in there, too, to make the skin firm.)

"When the razor gets full of shaving cream, I rinse it under the faucet.

"When shaving my neck, I point my chin upward to stretch the skin nice and tight. I usually shave in downward strokes because it's awkward for me to turn the razor around to shave upward, although I think other people do this (in order to shave against the direction in which beard hairs grow).

"I try not to press too hard because when I do, I accidentally cut myself.

"I'm extra careful near my earlobes and nostrils because the sensitive skin in these areas is easily nicked or cut if I'm not paying attention."

### FYI Cologne

If you want to, you can use cologne, but don't skunk up the place.

A little bit is good. Some people feel that none is even better!

## Disposable (Throwaway) Razors

Disposable razors are popular and relatively safe to use, although it is easy with any razor to nick or cut yourself while shaving. Disposable razors should not be used more than a few times—they get dull.

Through trial and error, you can pick the brand of disposable razor that works best for you; many guys recommend double-bladed or triple-bladed. The more blades, the better.

Razors should not be shared. Although it would be very unlikely to become exposed to blood-borne disease through a shared razor blade, it is technically possible (see page 89).

### HEADS UP! Ingrown Hairs

Sometimes whiskers bend at the tips, arch downward, and puncture the skin. These irritations cause pimples to form.

There are shaving techniques that can help avoid this recurring problem. One trick is not to get too close a shave. You may need to use a single-bladed razor (rather than a double- or triple-bladed one) or an electric shaver.

Talk to your doctor or dermatologist.

## KEEPING THE UPHOLSTERY CLEAN

Your clothes need to be relatively clean for you to stay smelling good.

Ask for a lesson on how to use your washing machine. Here are the basics for beginners:

1. Don't stuff it full of clothes, you'll break it. It's better to do an extra load or two than it is to overload the washer and burn out the motor. Also, your clothes will get cleaner.

2. Check the washing machine settings. Don't run a full load on a low water cycle. There has to be enough water! Use the normal setting, unless you're washing clothes marked delicate on the labels.

3. Let some water run in first and dissolve a measured amount of detergent in the water before adding the clothes. Read instructions on the detergent box or bottle.

4. Balance the load—arrange evenly around the agitator. Otherwise, the washing machine will shake, rattle, and hop around the floor and possibly break.

5. Wash dark clothes with other dark clothes and lights with lights.

6. Check every label for washing instructions and follow them.

7. Check every label for drying instructions and follow them. This is critical!

Tip: If you take your clothes out of the dryer, flap or smooth 'em out and fold or hang them when still warm, they'll be less wrinkled.

If you stuff warm clothes into a laundry basket all balled up, they'll end up totally wrinkled!

8. Don't do other family members' laundry without their permission. It's so easy to ruin clothes during the washing/drying process.

## Bleach

Don't mix bleach with other household chemicals! Lethal gases can form as a result.

Okay to use it in the washer along with standard laundry detergent, unless the directions say otherwise.

Begin the cycle that fills the washing machine with water. Once the washer is partly filled, carefully measure and add bleach to the water (don't just guess and glug it in) before putting in your clothes.

Do this before the agitator starts so you won't get clobbered by the agitator.

If not properly and evenly diluted with water, bleach will make splotchy marks and even weaken the fabric and make holes in it!

Basically, bleach is for white stuff. It makes clothes whiter and gets out certain stains.

Don't use bleach unless you've checked every label of everything you are going to wash. Lots of white clothes can't be bleached successfully.

## HEADS UP!

Make sure you don't get bleach in your eyes, and if you do, immediately start rinsing them under a gentle stream of water (cup your hands and blink into the water as it flows) and keep on rinsing them for 15 minutes. Then call your doctor.

Meanwhile, if someone is home, have that person call your doctor, poison control, or the local emergency room for you and ask what else to do.

## Got no washer/dryer?

If you don't have access to a washing machine, routinely wash out your underwear and socks in the bathroom sink or tub—with warm water and a bar of soap. Rinse well.

The Foolproof Drying Procedure: Lay the article of clothing (T-shirt, for example) on a towel, tightly roll the towel up, and then wring it as hard as you can. Then unroll the towel, flap out the shirt, and hang the shirt (and towel) up to dry.

## Hamper Violations

Prowling through the dirty clothes hamper and sniff-testing your T-shirts as a kind of rotation method of selecting your outfit for the day is an absolute infraction.

## Skid Marks

Skid marks keep showing up in your underwear?

These can be mighty unpleasant for whoever does the wash—including you. Plus, they stain.

Bathroom tip: Wipe and look at the toilet paper. If it's clean, wash your hands and you're outta there. Otherwise, keep at it.

## Another Bathroom Tip:

There's a handy little device in every bathroom called a toilet paper holder. When the roll gets down to the cardboard cylinder, be a good guy: Replace it!

**HEADS UP!**

Wash your hands with soap and lots of water after you use the bathroom—especially after you poop. Poop has *E. coli* bacteria in it and other germs that can make people really sick! Also: Baby in the house? Wash up carefully after changing or handling a poopy diaper.

It's always important to be on poop patrol—but it's especially important before preparing and eating food.

## Keeping Fluid Levels in Check

Deodorants (cover odor)/antiperspirants (block perspiration) are available in various forms: spray, cream, stick (solid), and roll-on. They all work pretty much the same. Some are scented, some aren't. If you're not sure which kind you want, it's safe to buy an unscented stick or roll-on deodorant. That way, you won't end up with one that smells too strong or has a scent you don't like.

Deodorants are sold all over the place; you're certain to find them sold in drugstores, grocery stores, and convenience stores. They cost about $3 or $4 each—maybe a little more. But a deodorant lasts quite a long time.

There's usually a men's section and a women's section of deodorants. They all work the same, but the women's types often have scents associated with girls—like "spring bouquets," for example. The guy ones have more "masculine" scents—whatever that means. Regardless, they're clearly labeled. Some are unisex. And again—many, both for men and women, are unscented.

To use deodorant, take off the cap and roll it around under each armpit for a few seconds.

If you're going to put on a dress shirt, you may want to wait a minute before putting the shirt on after using deodorant. That way, the deodorant will have a chance to dry and won't show up on the fabric. (A deodorant marked "clear" is the least likely to transfer onto your clothing when you're getting dressed.)

A good time to put on deodorant is after a shower—after you dry off and cool off a little. If you do it that way, it usually lasts all day, unless you become involved in a raucous game or sporting event.

If you shower at night before bed, it isn't necessary to put on deodorant. Just put it on in the morning.

## Phantom Deodorant

With stick-type deodorants you have to occasionally dispense a little more deodorant for yourself by turning the bottom of the container. If you don't move it up, you'll just be rubbing the applicator onto your armpit without any deodorant going on.

➤ **TIP:**
You may want to keep an extra deodorant in your pack, locker, or gym bag—especially if your PE class is scheduled early in the day.

# ROUTINE SERVICING
## Getting a Physical Exam

If you haven't had a routine physical (checkup) lately, now might be a good time to make an appointment to schedule one.

➤ **WORRIED?**
Worried about starting puberty too early or too late? Have other concerns about your changing body?

You're probably doing just fine, but why make yourself miserable stressing about it?

Evaluation of growth and development is an important part of a physical exam for a kid.

If someone actually is way too far ahead or behind in beginning puberty, it's possible to slow down or speed up the process.

These would be very rare situations, since the normal range is such a wide one!

A checkup is different from a visit to the doctor for an earache or a sore throat. It's a special appointment (usually done once a year) during which a doctor or other qualified health care provider spends time looking at "the whole picture," such as your height, your weight, your vision, and whether all your immunizations are up to date. A physical checkup for a growing boy also includes checking his blood pressure and the general condition of his heart, lungs, and abdomen. It includes having a doctor check the boy's penis and testicles to make sure they're up to snuff.

A checkup provides a good opportunity to talk with a doctor about changes that may be going on in your body. If you have questions, you can ask them and get answers. It's appropriate for you to ask to talk privately with your doctor if you feel you want or need to. This means: no mom or dad in the room, if that's the way you want it.

It's a good idea to write your questions down before the appointment so you won't forget to ask them.

It is also a good time to talk with your doctor about problems you may be having at home, in school, or with friends.

Be honest with your doctor if he (or she) asks you questions, even embarrassing ones. Your health care provider may need to know information that you may consider private, in order to take good care of you. This includes information about sexual contacts you may have had.

Also, don't withhold information from your doctor about drug and alcohol use and/or abuse. A doctor needs to be aware of all drugs a patient is using, including illegal drugs and over-the-counter drugs.

You don't need to wait for a checkup to talk to a doctor if something is troubling you.

# CHASSIS CHECKS YOUR FRAME
## Scoliosis

Sometimes, as a kid begins to enter puberty, his (or her) spine starts to grow faster than it should, and it begins to curve. This is called scoliosis, and in most cases, the problems associated with it can be avoided if a doctor becomes aware of it early. Scoliosis is one of many important reasons to have routine physical checkups.

Many school districts have programs in which the school nurse checks kids for scoliosis. Having your back checked for scoliosis doesn't hurt at all.

# BLURRY WINDSHIELD?
## Eye Exams

A brief eye test (reading an eye chart) is part of a routine checkup. Be sure to tell your doctor and/or parents if you have trouble seeing the chalkboard at school, if movies seem blurry, or if it's difficult to read books and magazines.

Your school may also offer eye testing. A teacher, a teacher's aide, the principal, or the school nurse may be able to help schedule an eye exam for you at school.

Some kids (and adults) are self-conscious at first about wearing glasses, but being able to see clearly more than makes up for it. Like anything new, it takes a while to adjust to wearing glasses—but after a short time, it's no big deal.

If you are interested in contact lenses, listen carefully to what your eye doctor has to say about them. Leave contacts in only for the recommended length of time. Also, follow all instructions on cleaning your contacts. This is really important to help prevent eye infections and injuries.

## Dental Exams

Dentists recommend that kids have dental checkups twice a year. Teeth need to be cleaned in a dentist's office routinely in order to avoid cavities and maintain good health of the gums.

Brushing and flossing do make a difference; brush as soon as you can after every meal. Use fluoride toothpaste, especially if your water is not fluoridated. Chewing sugarless gum helps flush the teeth with saliva and may help prevent cavities, but brushing is better.

### Smelly Emissions

Bad breath can be an indication of having a dental problem.

Don't avoid contacting a dentist if you get a toothache; a toothache may be an indication that you have a cavity (hole) in one of your teeth, which will just become bigger and bigger until it is filled. Untreated cavities can make dental treatment complicated and expensive. Decaying teeth may also pose additional health risks.

Do you have questions about getting hooked up with affordable dental care? You or your parent can begin by talking to the county health department, listed in the phone book.

Perhaps your school nurse has some additional information.

## THE GRILL
### Orthodontic Exams

A dentist may recommend that you make an appointment with an orthodontist. An orthodontist is a dentist who corrects irregularities of the bite. The orthodontist will evaluate whether or not you actually need braces.

Not every family can afford braces just for the purpose of designing the perfect smile. They're very expensive! However, it's usually possible to straighten your teeth or improve your bite when you're an adult, if you still want to by the time you grow up.

You don't have to have straight teeth to have a great-looking smile, though—and not every adult wants perfectly straight teeth. Neither does every kid.

Keep on smiling: crooked teeth, braces, and all.

What's behind the smile is what matters most: you!

# CHAPTER 4

# OPERATING INSTRUCTIONS:
## KEEPING THE SYSTEMS
# RUNNING
## *Smoothly*

## FILLING THE TANK: FOOD AND YOUR HEALTH

Everyone's body needs food to perform properly. A healthy diet includes appropriate combinations of proteins, fats, carbohydrates, and all of the vitamins and minerals required by the body. A well-balanced diet can be achieved by eating a variety of fruits and vegetables, low-fat dairy products, whole-grain cereals and breads, and lean red meat, chicken, fish, beans, nuts, and legumes.

Those who choose to eat a vegetarian diet must be extra careful to meet nutritional needs — especially during puberty, when the body is growing and changing very rapidly. Before deciding to eliminate meat and/or dairy from your diet, consult a health care professional. You'll need to be completely clear on how to fulfill your daily requirements, especially in the protein, iron, B vitamins, and calcium departments.

### *Fill 'er up!*

Try not to skip meals—especially breakfast!

Kids who don't eat breakfast don't perform as well as they could in school. If you skip breakfast, it means that your body has had to go all night and then all the next morning until lunch to get the nourishment it needs. This can make you feel weak, irritable, sick, unable to concentrate, down in the dumps, and disinterested in your schoolwork.

At least eat a bowl of cereal (with low-fat or skim milk) in the morning. And grab a banana or an apple on your way out the door!

### *Do you like drinking milk?*

If not, eat yogurt, frozen yogurt, cottage cheese, or other dairy products (nonfat and low-fat varieties are available). Your bones are still growing, gaining as much as 4 inches a year, and you need lots of calcium, which is found in milk products, to achieve your genetic potential for height and build strong bones.

If you don't "do dairy," you can get calcium from calcium-fortified juices, cereals, and other foods.

# Food Guide Pyramid
## A Guide to Daily Food Choices

Fats, Oils &
Sweets
**USE SPARINGLY**

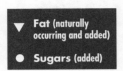

▼ **Fat** (naturally
occurring and added)

● **Sugars** (added)

Milk, Yogurt &
Cheese Group
**2–3 SERVINGS**

Meat, Poultry,
Fish, Dry Beans,
Eggs & Nuts
Group
**2–3 SERVINGS**

Vegetable Group
**3–5 SERVINGS**

Fruit Group
**2–4 SERVINGS**

Bread, Cereal,
Rice & Pasta
Group
**6–11
SERVINGS**

### WHAT COUNTS AS A SERVING?

**Bread, Cereal, Rice, and Pasta Group**
• 1 slice of bread
• About 1 cup of ready-to-eat cereal
• ½ cup of cooked cereal, rice, or pasta

**Vegetable Group**
• 1 cup of raw leafy vegetables
• ½ cup of other vegetables—cooked or raw
• ¾ cup of vegetable juice

**Fruit Group**
• 1 medium apple, banana, orange, or pear
• ½ cup of chopped, cooked, or canned fruit in natural juices
• ¾ cup of fruit juice

**Milk, Yogurt, and Cheese Group**
• 1 cup of milk* or yogurt*
• 1½ oz. of natural cheese*
• 2 oz. of processed cheese*

**Meat, Poultry, Fish, Dry Beans, Eggs, and Nuts Group**
• 2–3 oz. of cooked lean meat, poultry, or fish
• ½ cup of cooked dry beans** or ½ cup of tofu counts as 1 oz. of lean meat
• 2 tbsp. of peanut butter or ⅓ cup of nuts counts as 1 oz. of meat

*Choose fat-free or reduced-fat dairy products most often.   **Dry beans, peas, and lentils can be counted as servings in either meat and beans group or the vegetable group.

---

But be vigilant! If you cannot get enough from food, talk to your health care provider about taking calcium supplements.

### Lactose Intolerance

If you are lactose-intolerant (have difficulty digesting the sugar present in milk properly), your pediatrician can help you to make appropriate substitutions for milk in your diet and/or suggest a medication to help with digestion. Calcium supplements may be advised.

### Other good sources of calcium include...

. . . canned fish with soft bones such as sardines, anchovies, and salmon; dark green leafy vegetables such as kale, mustard greens, turnip greens, and bok choy; tofu, if processed with calcium sulfate (read labels); tortillas made from lime-processed corn (read labels).

### A daily multivitamin pill with minerals...

. . . is a good idea for a growing kid. You don't have to buy expensive ones; just standard daily multiple vitamins from the drugstore or grocery store work.

### Do you shop for yourself?
If so, here's a handy list of what to buy.

## SHOPPING LIST OF NUTRITIOUS, LOW-FAT FOODS

**Fruits and Vegetables and Legumes**

Apples
Apricots
Bananas
Bok choy
Broccoli
Brussels sprouts
Cabbage
Cantaloupe
Carrots
Cauliflower
Chickpeas
Dried beans
(navy beans, pinto beans,
black beans, etc.)
Kale
Melons
Oranges
Peaches
Pears
Potatoes
Prunes
Raisins
Raspberries
Red and green peppers
Spinach
Strawberries
Sweet potatoes
Tomatoes
Winter squash

**Animal Products**

Cheese (made from skim milk)
Chicken/turkey (remove skin)
Fish
Lean meats (trim fat)
Milk (nonfat/low-fat)
Yogurt (nonfat/low-fat)

**Cereals and Grains**

Brown rice
Corn tortillas
Pasta
Whole-grain bread
Whole-grain cereals

Source: American Cancer Society.

## High-Octane Fuel

How much fast food do you eat?

Fast food, like cheeseburgers and fries, has a higher fat and calorie content than you may need on a regular basis. Be moderate in your consumption of fast food.

Fresh food—like fresh fruits and vegetables— and food that's prepared by baking, broiling, boiling, steaming, poaching, and grilling is generally more healthy than food that's prepared by frying, especially deep-fat frying.

## Read the Map

Most fast-food restaurants offer heathful options: green salad, frozen yogurt with fruit topping, roasted chicken, tostadas piled with lettuce, tomatoes, onions, and beans. . . . Check out the menu!

Extra-large fries, huge soft drinks—and all for just a few cents more? Maybe it's best just to pass on these offers.

## Snacks

Choose healthy snacks, like popcorn and fruit. Sweet between meal snacks promote tooth decay—especially chewy, sticky sweet snacks. If you can't resist them, brush after you eat them. If you can't brush, rinse your mouth with water. It at least helps!

## Drinks

Sweetened drinks (like sodas, for example) have amazing amounts of added sugar—say, 12 teaspoons or more per drink. Experts in nutrition are beginning to advise us to pretty much give sweetened drinks the boot. They're considered one of the primary causes of **obesity** (being very fat).

**HEADS UP!**
"Nutraceutical" drinks promise health benefits, but a lot of claims are false. Some of the herbal additives can be straight-up bad for you!

## Worried about being too light or too heavy?

Pediatricians are trained to evaluate growth, and a visit to discuss your weight can be very reassuring. Being slim usually isn't a medical problem at all, but it can be, especially if you are severely underweight.

Obesity is a growing problem in the United States. What makes it complicated is the fact that eating and body-image disorders are also problems! We don't want to focus too much on weight.

But you do need to pay attention to it so that you remain in the healthy weight range.

Our convenience-oriented culture, coupled with easy access to high-fat, high-calorie foods and the availability of fun things to do that just involve sitting, has contributed to a rise in obesity of teens.

If you think you're overweight, talk to your pediatrician. He or she can decide what is a healthy weight range for you. If he or she agrees that slowing your weight gain, maintaining your weight, or losing weight is a healthy choice for you, you can map out a program together.

Weight management for kids in puberty should be supervised by a health care professional who can recommend a specific nutritional/active-lifestyle program. In puberty, when you are growing and changing so fast, your body requires lots of specific nutrients.

Or you can ask for a referral to a registered dietitian, who can help you evaluate your eating habits and daily intake of food and advise you as to changes you may make regarding food choices. And follow your progress!

Your registered dietitian (or doctor) may also help you devise an exercise plan that fits your lifestyle and is workable for you.

Eat better. Be less inactive. Be more active. But . . .

## Don't diet.

It's true that we can all live without that huge piece of cake or pie or that double-scoop ice cream cone or extra blob of butter and generous dollop of sour cream on a baked potato.

And yes, we can choose to eat a few cookies or chips rather than a whole stack. Or better yet, substitute fruit for cookies and chips.

But don't diet.

Diets, including fad diets, just plain don't work in the long run. They may even disrupt your normal metabolic rate and be counterproductive for weight loss. And dieting can be detrimental to the health of growing teens.

It's fine to cut back on or eliminate stuff—like sweetened drinks, candy, and desserts, for example—that has little or no redeeming nutritional value.

A switch from whole-milk products (milk, ice cream, cheese) to nonfat or low-fat milk products is also a fine idea. Nobody needs the quantities of saturated fats (bad fats, which clog the arteries) that are present in whole milk and other dairy and animal products.

It's also fine to cut back on portion sizes at meals.

### HEADS UP!

A registered dietitian or otherwise qualified professional should be involved in any athletic program for teens that stresses weight loss or gain as part of training or competing. Look into it. Wrestlers: This means you!

## PARKING VIOLATIONS

Failure to move around enough is one cause of weight gain. Odd as it sounds, prolonged TV watching is fattening. It's often coupled with turbo-snacking and intense exposure to ads for high-calorie, high-fat food. To get fit or stay fit, you may need to reduce the amount of time you

# CHEF TIPS

Cooking for yourself or your family? Here are some tips for safe handling and preparation of food:

Separate raw, cooked, and ready-to-eat foods while shopping, preparing, and storing. This prevents cross-contamination. (Example: Bacteria present in raw chicken gets onto salad stuff when juice drips out of the package.)

Don't put cooked or ready-to-eat food on any surface, plate, pan, or bowl (or utensil) that has come in contact with raw meat, raw poultry, raw seafood, or raw egg—unless the surface (or plate, etc.) has been washed with hot, soapy water. Barbecuers beware!

Don't leave perishable food out of the refrigerator for more than 2 hours—1 hour if the air temperature is above 90° F.

Defrost frozen food in the refrigerator, microwave, under cold running water, or in cold water changed every 30 minutes.

Marinate food in the refrigerator.

Cook food to proper temperature. Thermometers designed to test the temperatures of food can be bought at the grocery store. Just make sure you follow instructions on the package.

Make sure the microwave heats food evenly. Cover, turn, and stir, if necessary. Follow the instructions on the packaging.

Divide large amounts of leftovers into small, shallow containers for quick cooling in the refrigerator.

Don't stuff that refrigerator! Air needs to circulate for the system to work right.

Wash your hands for 20 seconds (count to 30) with warm, soapy water before handling food (or utensils) and after handling raw meat, poultry, fish, shellfish, and eggs.

Wash fruits and vegetables before eating.

Want to know more? Call 1-888-SAFE FOOD or visit www.foodsafety.gov.

|  |  |
|---|---|
| 180°F | Whole Poultry |
| 170°F | Poultry Breast, Well-Done Meats |
| 165°F | Stuffing, Ground Poultry, Reheated Leftovers |
| 160°F | Medium Meats, Raw Eggs, Egg Dishes, Pork, and Ground Meats |
| 145°F | Medium-Rare Beef Steaks, Roasts, Veal, Lamb |
| 140°F | Hold Hot Foods |
|  | DANGER ZONE for Bacterial Growth |
| 40°F | Refrigerator Temperatures |
| 0°F | Freezer Temperatures |

spend sitting in neutral in front of the computer or TV. Adolescent health experts recommend 2 hours daily, max.

### Check the meter.

Once you figure out how many hours a day you spend just sitting, you can make an adjustment. Set some limits for yourself.

### Just do stuff.

You may think I'm working for your parents when I say this, but listen up: Lounging around burns way fewer calories than doing just about anything else (except sleeping, maybe).

Unloading the groceries, putting them away, vacuuming, sweeping, gardening, raking leaves, shoveling snow, organizing the garage, cleaning up your room—all these annoying chores assigned to you by your parents help keep you fit without your even leaving your home.

➤ Identify the physical activities that you like doing and do them all year-round.
It's best to build activity into your everyday routine.

### HEADS UP!
If you are extremely overweight, check with your doctor before stepping up your activity level. Team up and make a plan. You can do this!

### Have fun.

Participate in sports if you want to. If you don't, get some exercise in other ways.

Keep alternative sports in mind. If you don't like football, so what! Lots of guys reject football and other team sports. Play Ping-Pong!

Maybe it's nerdy—but it's a blast!

Play croquet!

Not good at it?

Be bad at it!

Just have fun.

Don't like games?

Noncompetitive activities that stress participation rather than winning may be the way for you to go.

### HEADS UP!

Moderate exercise that focuses on strength, flexibility, and cardiovascular health is the key to creating and maintaining a balance for total fitness. To avoid injury, even a moderate workout should include stretching, warming up, exercising, cooling down, and stretching again. Find out how before you start!

## Community Fitness Programs for Teens

Just about every community has supervised programs to keep teens fit and active—and occupied. The cost is usually low or free. Ask your parent or teacher to help you find what's available. Depending on where you live, you may be able to sign up for anything from basketball to ballroom dancing, from karate to yoga.

## Water Ahead

Health clubs, country clubs, and backyard pools are the greatest, but we don't all have access to these terrific places.

If you don't, remember: Many communities do have a YMCA or other public facility where you can take lessons and swim for a reasonable fee or for free.

Why not call and check it out?

Go first with your parent or other trusted adult to scope out the situation. And never swim alone. Buddy up!

## Just dance f-a-s-t.

Dancing fast is great exercise and fun all at the same time. You don't need a partner. Dance with the doorknob; dance with yourself in the mirror if you want.

## Just go for a walk!

If you're in good health, walking briskly is great for physical fitness.

Unfortunately, we don't all have access to a beautiful walking path through a safe neighborhood. If you don't, choose another fitness activity. If you do—cool! Still, don't walk alone. And walk where someone could be called upon for help if needed (see page 136).

When you're out in the world, remain aware of your surroundings. Leave your disc player at home. Wear something bright so you're visible from a distance. Don't walk at dusk or in the dark.

## Off-Roading

Does your parent or other adult relative like to hike?

Hiking in the out-of-doors may be the single most satisfying form of exercise if you love nature, but don't hike alone. Kids should hike with a responsible adult. A *short* hike on a well-marked trail is the way to begin.

## Check it out.

Any marked hiking trails in the parks in your area? First, let your fingers do the walking: Use the phone book to find out. (Try looking under government listings under county, state, or national parks.) Ask when the park opens and closes and what trails are for beginners. Are maps provided? Where do you get one? It's best to hike with a trail map. Ask if there are any particular hazards you need to be aware of, like poisonous snakes or poison oak, ivy, or sumac.

Plan to stay on the trail. Scrambling around on rocks or on steep terrain or going cross-country should be avoided, unless you are hiking with an experienced adult guide.

High-tech equipment is the greatest, but if you don't own hiking boots, a sturdy pair of high-topped sneakers that support your ankles and feet and have good treads—and a small day pack—will be great for starters (on a beginners' trail). Bring a hat with a brim and sunglasses. Don't forget sunscreen.

Throw into your backpack a couple of plastic bottles of water. You'll need to drink plenty while you're on the trail, but don't expect to be able to drink from streams or lakes along the way. Unfortunately, most are contaminated.

Bring a healthy, high-calorie snack that doesn't spoil easily in your pack, such as trail mix, a couple of energy bars, and/or a peanut-butter-and-jelly sandwich or two. Oranges are also great to carry along, since they don't squash easily. And they're so refreshing! Empty a little water out of one of the bottles (so the bottle won't break) and freeze it; it will keep your food cool. Remember perishable food needs to be eaten within 2 hours, or 1 hour if the air temperature is above 90°F. Toss in a flashlight and a couple of extra batteries (it's a very good idea to hike with a flashlight no matter what time you expect to be home), a pack of matches or plastic lighter sealed in a plastic bag,

## GO EASY ON YOURSELF

Achieving the "look" of a model is not a practical or meaningful goal for boys or girls. Accepting ourselves and each other, including our different body types, is.

People are genetically programmed to be a variety of sizes and shapes. Clothing ads, especially those featured in teen or fashion magazines, are famous for portraying unrealistic images of both men and women.

Photos of models in ads are often "enhanced" (faked); the photo's touched up. We see the same male body type over and over again in ads: tall, broad-shouldered, slender, very buff.

Certain models, entertainers, and actors have had plastic (cosmetic) surgery to achieve the "perfect" body; some guys even have biceps implants.

Many women in film, TV, and print ads may have had breast-implant surgery, "tummy tucks," butt lifts, rib removal, or liposuction (surgical fat-cell removal). Many struggle with eating disorders to try to maintain an unnaturally thin body.

Only a small percentage of girls will grow up to have the size and shape of breasts, hips, and thighs commonly seen on models wearing swimsuits, lingerie, or low-cut dresses; only a small percentage of guys will grow up to be proportioned like models.

It's reassuring to take a look around at the people you know—or even see walking around.

Most people, regardless of age, just look like people—not actors or supermodels.

and something warm in case the weather cools off. A pocketknife can come in handy, too.

A few Band-Aids are helpful in case you develop blisters on the trail. Are ticks or mosquitoes a problem? If so, use and bring repellent.

A wad of toilet paper or tissues is essential.

Now get your adult onto his or her feet—and you're on your way. Stretch before you start hiking and warm up by walking slowly for the first few minutes.

Hiking opens up amazing possibilities. Photography and bird watching are two of them, to say nothing of beginning a lifelong love affair with nature.

**HEADS UP!**
If your school pack is doubling as your day pack for hiking, make sure you take out your matches/lighter and pocketknife before going back to school with it.

## FOCUSING ON THE EXTERIOR
*Set and maintain reasonable standards for yourself.*

There are good reasons to eat a nutritious, moderate-fat diet (with good fats) and to exercise regularly. It's appropriate to have the goals of being healthy, strong, and in good shape. But remember: You don't have to be buff to be physically fit. Only a handful of people are genetically programmed to be able to achieve the body of a professional athlete or Olympian. If you think you've got what it takes to become one of the few—go for it!

### Consumer Alert

The media have invented an idealized male image that can cause some guys to feel as though they just don't "measure up." Preteen and teen boys are particularly vulnerable to these feelings. If you learn how to "read the media," you will recognize that many commercials are designed to make us feel like we're just, somehow, not good enough the way we are—that we need to buy something (which they're promoting) to be popular, successful, and powerful.

### Bodybuilding

Dream of having big biceps and a six-pack?

For the moment, your body is busy building itself.

Talk to your doctor before embarking on a program to increase your muscle mass.

He or she will want to identify what stage of puberty you are in before advising you as to when and if it's okay for you to start bodybuilding (if you start too early, you can conceivably work against your own natural, healthy muscular development).

Likewise, before taking nutritional supplements (including herbal supplements) to gain or lose weight, run the products past your doctor, regardless of the safety claims on the container or what the salesperson promises you.

Unregulated nutritional supplements can be dangerous. There have been problems regarding quality control and contamination of supplement ingredients.

It's also hard to know what quantities (or combinations) might actually be bad for your health. And please keep this in mind: Just because something is labeled "natural" or "herbal" doesn't mean it's good for you.

### Don't take steroids!

Unless they are prescribed by your physician to address a medical problem, don't take steroids.

**HEADS UP!**
Among other things, steroids can permanently damage the heart, cause dangerous mood

swings, and interfere with sexual drive and response.

Sharing needles used to inject steroids is one way people become infected with blood-borne germs such as HIV—the virus that causes AIDS (see page 88).

## Be aware of eating disorders.

Focusing too much on body image may foreshadow the development of an actual eating disorder.

An eating disorder is an illness that causes someone to abuse himself or herself. Purposely starving, exercising way too much and too often, taking drugs for the purpose of speeding up the natural process of pooping and peeing, and binge-eating and/or throwing up on purpose to lose weight or to avoid gaining weight are all potential symptoms of eating disorders.

It's fine—in fact, good—to be aware of the nutritional content of the food you eat. Paying attention to nutrition facts labels is a good thing to do. But becoming obsessed with calorie counting and consumed by counting grams of fat are also signs that a preteen or teen may be developing a negative relationship with food and may be at risk for developing an eating disorder.

### HEADS UP!

Anorexia nervosa is a condition in which a person restricts food intake too much and falls dangerously below his or her ideal body-weight range.

Bulimia is a condition in which a person regularly binges on food, then starves or uses laxatives or vomiting to avoid putting on weight.

Excessive exercising is a form of an eating disorder in which the person exercises for hours and hours every day to burn calories to lose weight.

## Blind Spots

Often a person with an eating disorder does not recognize or admit that he or she has this problem. In fact, he or she hides the problem—or tries to. Denial of the problem may be a symptom of the disorder.

Eating disorders can inhibit normal growth and development and damage to the body, including the heart, skeleton, and brain. Many people succumb to the illness completely and die.

With help from health care professionals, it's possible to overcome the illness before irreversible damage occurs. A number of *very* effective medications are now available to help with the process of recovering.

Do you have questions about yourself, a sibling, or a friend?

Talk to a parent, doctor, teacher, or counselor.

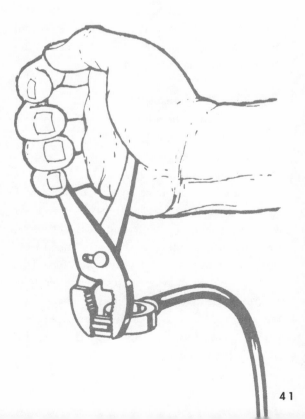

# CHAPTER 5

# INTERIOR
## *Care:*
## WHEN THE ROAD GETS ROUGH

## A MAN AIN'T MADE OF STEEL

Face it: Boys are often discouraged from expressing (and feeling) certain emotions, such as sadness, fear, and anxiety.

But we need to get real with each other.

Everybody experiences feelings of sadness, vulnerability, loneliness, fear, anxiety, shame, and confusion at one time or another.

### *The Gender Conflict*

The redefining of the roles of men and women can be a source of confusion for all of us.

Especially adolescent boys!

Here's the prob:

Historically, boys have been encouraged to be tough, strong, protective, aggressive, competitive, and independent. Right or wrong, these characteristics have been linked with being "masculine."

But hmmm. In recent years, boys have been encouraged to be more open, to share their feelings, and to be sensitive to the feelings of others. Males are now called upon to take on more active roles in parenting and homemaking—roles that have historically been reserved for women.

Girls can experience similar confusion. Our culture signals to girls that they're supposed to be dependent and in many ways weak, to be "feminine." At the same time, we encourage girls to be strong, assertive, competitive, and independent. And why not?

Why should these powerful traits be associated exclusively with males?

The roles of men and women have been continuously changing over the past few decades; it's okay to feel confused. But at least be sure of this much:

Both boys and girls (and men and women) feel all ways: strong and weak, powerful and vulnerable, confident and insecure, courageous and afraid.

These are human feelings. They're not attached to a particular gender.

### *Circuit Breakers*

Talking about troublesome feelings with someone you trust and love makes having the feelings less painful. It also builds strong, healthy friendships and family relationships.

It's good to rely on your parents for emotional support and comfort. Letting your parents back you

up will make you stronger and more powerful as an adult, not weaker.

### Mama's Boy?

You better believe it! It's outdated and old-fashioned (and sexist!) to believe that having strong communication with your mom will make you less of a male.

For starters, women can be just as tough, strong, assertive, and competitive as men. Some of the strongest men on earth have had women watching their backs.

More important, moms (like dads) understand the pressure boys are up against out in the world. They're also good at teaching boys the skills they need to grow into confident adults.

So many boys don't have a dad in their lives! Whether you do or don't, keep on hanging out with your mom; it's good for you. Chances are she's been there for some other guys, too. Like your dad, step-dad, uncle, or grandpa.

Why shouldn't she be there for you?

### On Overload

Not all troublesome feelings or conflicts can be resolved by talking about them with your family and friends. If you are troubled by sad, worried, or anxious feelings that don't go away or keep coming back again, ask for help. If your emotions seem out of control, ask for help.

You can get help by asking your parents, doctor, teacher, or school counselor — or another adult you trust — to help you find a psychologist, psychiatrist, or counselor. Or you can call the county health department for a referral. (Ask the information operator [411] or look under county

government listings in the phone book.)

Or you can call a youth crisis hot line (see page 46). Call 911 or another police emergency number in any health emergency, including a mental health emergency.

## Mental Health Care

Doctors and other adults are aware of the stress that can accompany adolescence, and just about every community has mental health care available for children and teens. Mental health care may include medication used in combination with therapy. Outstanding new medications have been developed for depression, anxiety, eating disorders, panic disorders, and other conditions.

Therapy is a process that involves talking and listening. With guidance from a trained health care provider, we can explore and identify what is making us feel bad and work through the problem. As the problem is resolved, positive thoughts and good feelings may replace the negative, sad ones.

It isn't necessary to feel sad, scared, anxious, or "out of control" to get counseling or help. Lots of people talk to mental health care professionals to gain insight and improve coping skills. Getting therapy doesn't mean you're crazy or can't help yourself. It enables you to understand your life better and feel more in control of it.

## Drugs, Alcohol, and Stress

Some people may use illegal drugs or alcohol to try to manage stress or other uncomfortable or painful feelings. Although some of these substances may seem to offer temporary relief, they're actually harmful to emotional well-being and physical health.

## Suicide Threats

If anyone talks to you about wanting to end his or her own life, tell a parent, a teacher, the school prin-

cipal, a counselor, a health care professional, a police officer, or another adult you trust. Tell right away, even if you promised your friend you wouldn't tell. Don't try to decide whether or not the person might actually attempt suicide—all threats of suicide must be taken seriously. A person thinking about suicide should not be left alone.

**HEADS UP!**
**Remember: In any emergency, call 911 or another police emergency number.**

If you yourself have suicidal thoughts or feelings, tell your parent or another trusted adult such as a doctor, or teacher. And if you think you might act on these feelings, tell right away. Suicide is completely preventable. Depression is treatable. The trouble with depression is that it can feel like it will never end. But that's not true. There are many treatments that can help depression.

There are different causes of depression, including having a chemical imbalance in the brain. Depression can also be caused by real issues that teenagers have to deal with. There are so many medications available that can help you achieve a more positive, upbeat outlook on life! And counseling or therapy can help you identify and explore the source(s) of your desperate feelings—and do something to change them.

**HEADS UP! Help is out there.**
**Suicide prevention hot lines are available 24-7. National Hope Line 1-800-SUICIDE (1-800-784-2433) or 1-888-SUICIDE (1-888-784-2433).**
**The Girls and Boys Town National Hot Line is also a suicide prevention hot line: 1-800-448-3000 (see page 46).**
**Other suicide prevention numbers can be found by dialing 411 or 0 and asking the operator.**

## *Youth Crisis Hot Lines*

Youth crisis hot lines are staffed by trained volunteers or professional counselors who help callers identify their problems, explore options, and develop a plan of action. They also offer referrals to community-based services, support groups, and even shelters, if necessary. You will find hot line numbers in the box below.

Sometimes hot line numbers change.

The front pages of the phone book often list hot line numbers along with other emergency numbers. Or you can call the information operator (411) or the regular operator (0) and ask for help in finding a hot line number that you need.

## RUNNING AWAY

Some kids experience situations such as abuse, a serious breakdown in communication with parents, conflicts within the family, or other stressful circumstances that make them feel as if they just can't cope if they remain at home.

## TWENTY-FOUR-HOUR EMERGENCY ROADSIDE ASSISTANCE

Dial **911** in most areas, or dial **0** for the operator and ask for help getting connected to the police emergency number. If you're on a cell phone, tell the emergency operator where you're calling from.

Also: The following hot lines are currently available for anyone to call, free, 24 hours a day. The call doesn't appear on your phone bill. Hang in there! It may be necessary to wait for a few moments for a counselor to come on the line.

**Covenant House Nine Line** (youth crisis line; call to talk about any problem): **1-800-999-9999** (U.S. only)

**National Runaway Switchboard** (youth crisis line for kids who are thinking about running away, for kids who have already run away, or for kids who want to talk about other problems):
**1-800-621-4000** (U.S. only)
For the hearing-impaired: **1-800-621-0394** (TTY)

**Child Help USA National Child Abuse Hot Line** (if there are concerns about physical, sexual, or emotional abuse or neglect):
**1-800-4-A-CHILD (1-800-422-4453)** (U.S. and Canada)
For the hearing-impaired: **1-800-2-A-CHILD (1-800-222-4453)** (TTY)

**Girls and Boys Town National Hot Line** (youth crisis line—to talk about any problem):
**1-800-448-3000** (U.S. and Canada)
For the hearing-impaired: **1-800-448-1833** (TTY)

**The National Center for Missing and Exploited Children (and Teens) Hot Line:**
**1-800-843-5678** (U.S. and Canada)
For the hearing-impaired: **1-800-826-7653** (TTY)

**National Hope Line 1-800-SUICIDE (1-800-784-2433)
or 1-888-SUICIDE (1-888-784-2433).**

**HEADS UP!**

Running away to the streets is not a solution; it exposes kids to crime and violence, hunger, disease, and people who prey on kids. All kids need to be able to count on an adult who will be responsible for them.

There are times when it is in a kid's best interest for alternate living arrangements to be made, on either a temporary or a permanent basis. These arrangements need to be made by responsible adults who are in a position to safeguard a child's health and welfare.

Social service agencies run by the government are equipped to handle these arrangements. These agencies and groups can be found by asking a school counselor, teacher, principal, or health care professional. They can also be found by looking in the phone book under government listings (turn to "county government" and look under "health services" and "social services") or by asking the information operator (411) for government social services listings.

They can also be found by getting a referral from a youth crisis hot line (see page 46).

In any emergency, including a mental health emergency, call 911 or the police emergency number for your area, or dial 0 and ask the operator for help.

Most problems can be solved by remaining at home, with support from trained professionals.

There are thousands of agencies and support groups set up to help kids and their families find safe solutions to problems by taking advantage of services within their own communities.

The above hot line calls are free. Anyone can call, and the call doesn't appear on the phone bill.

## Bullying

Bullying describes a form of aggression in which there is an intent to harm or intimidate somebody under circumstances where there is an imbalance of power. Over a period of time, a victim is made fearful by actions of one or several people.

Sexual harassment, rumor spreading, the taking of personal property, name calling, and teasing can occur in the context of bullying.

Some kids who are relentlessly bullied become depressed, anxious, and even suicidal. Who would want to make a kid that miserable?

**HEADS UP!**

Many bullies have underlying depression and/or other emotional problems—and need help. Believe it or not, bullying can be a roundabout way of asking for help.

## Get over it.

Accept people's differences. Let it go at that. The world isn't entirely made up of kids who look, think, and act the same.

What's cool about bullying? Nothing. Be part of the solution, not part of the problem. Don't reinforce the behavior of bullies by laughing with them or otherwise backing them up. Rewarding bullying perpetuates the problem.

Socially powerful kids can be known to charm adults (and teachers) on the one hand and bully kids on the other. If you become aware that bullying is going on unchecked at your school, find a teacher or counselor (privately, if you want) and discuss the situation—as you see it. Schools need to maintain a bully-free, safe atmosphere for everybody. Adults in charge may be unaware of bullying unless students come forward to tip them off.

## Feeling inclined to bully other kids?

Someone who experiences satisfaction in making other people miserable should identify why. Do you feel this way? If you do, ask your doctor to refer you to a counselor. Discover what's motivating or underlying your behavior so you can change it. You can find positive ways to use your power.

## Being bullied?

Begin by telling your parent(s). They can help you develop a plan for dealing with the situation. Want to talk to a counselor? Ask your doctor for a referral.

If you're being bullied at school, you (and your parents) can schedule a meeting with your school counselor or other school official to discuss your options.

Meanwhile:

The fact that someone has a problem with aggression doesn't mean there's something wrong with *you*; never forget that. Believe in your right to be yourself and in your right to ask for help from the adults around you. Remember, even if the bully is threatening to harm you if you tell (or harm someone else, like your little brother), you still need to tell a trusted adult if you are being bullied, no matter how scared you may be. It's okay to be afraid, but don't let the fear keep you from getting help.

# VIOLENCE
## Violence in the Media

When it comes to viewing violence as entertainment, our culture seems to have crossed the line.

Be aware of the issues:

Experts believe that viewing violent images over and over again tends to make people desensitized to violence. This means that we can become detached from the emotions that would normally accompany the witnessing of a violent act.

It's also suspected that children who view excessive amounts of violence on TV, in video games, and in the movies may themselves be at risk for becoming more aggressive.

> ➤ An eye for an eye, a tooth for a tooth? Forget it. This approach to conflict leaves no room for peaceful resolution.

## Imitating Fighting

Smashing people up against walls, kicking people in the face, head, neck, chest, or abdomen, strangling each other, breaking bottles over each other's heads, and so on is the kind of fighting most often modeled on TV and in the movies—where it's shown for entertainment.

In real life, these blows can kill people! People may also become paralyzed, sustain permanent brain damage, or suffer lifetime disabilities as a result of this kind of fighting.

## The Myth—
## You've Got to Fight to Be a Man

Sometimes people have to fight in self-defense. Under certain, specific circumstances, we can defend ourselves from physical attack, provided that we use no more force than is necessary to do so. If it's possible to retreat to safety from an attacker, we are expected to—and should.

But fighting just "to prove you're a man" is uncalled-for and can result in criminal charges being brought against you. So can using *excessive* force in self-defense (or defense of another).

Being a man involves realizing that it's okay to disagree, that conflict is a part of life, that disputes need not escalate to violence. It involves understanding anger and being aware of positive ways to express it. Being a man is about being able to keep anger in check. This means that unless you're lawfully defending yourself (or another), you've got to walk away from fights to be a man.

## Cooling System

Overheating in an argument or dispute—sound familiar?

Anger is often a reaction to the action(s) of others.

If you get mad at somebody, step back. Getting in somebody's face, or allowing them to get in yours, makes matters worse. Develop a cool-down system. Take a deep breath. Think for yourself. What kind of person do you want to be? Ask yourself: Do you want to be the kind of person who reacts violently? Get a grip on yourself. If necessary, walk completely away. There are many appropriate (even creative) ways to express anger. It may be helpful to talk to an adult. Communicating your feelings can help you think constructively about how you can deal positively with the situation.

## Releasing Steam
Physical activity is often effective in reducing levels of anger.

## Blowing a Gasket/Boiling Over
Rages are NOT uncontrollable. Help is available for anger management.

Your pediatrician or counselor can point you in the right direction for finding help with controlling your anger—before it starts to control you (and your future). Violence is a choice. You CAN make choices that do NOT involve violence.

With guidance from a qualified health care professional, you can learn to reduce levels of anger. You can learn effective coping behaviors to stop the escalation of angry feelings and to resolve conflicts without fighting. You can also gain a better understanding of the wide range of feelings that can come under the category of "mad" (including feeling sad, hurt, rejected, or stressed).

You can learn to control your thinking by identifying what "triggers" anger for you. You can learn how to avoid jumping to conclusions or demonizing the person you're mad at.

You can learn to set realistic standards for yourself and the people around you, so that you are less likely to get mad to begin with.

## Chill out.
Mmmmmmm. You can also acquire and use relaxation skills. Meditation, prayer, and yoga reduce stress for some people.

## Be a hero.
Tell your parent or another responsible adult if you become aware of a threat of violence. It isn't your job to try to figure out whether or not the person is serious.

## School Zone—Zero Tolerance
If you're aware (or even hear) that another kid is in possession of a gun or other lethal weapon at school, or has a plan to bring a gun or other lethal weapon to school, immediately tell a counselor, teacher, principal, or other responsible adult. Or call 911 or the police emergency number (anonymously, if you want).

You don't have to know whether or not the threat is serious—in fact, you can't know if the threat is real or if someone is playing a joke. So don't try to find out.

Just tell a responsible adult. This is the courageous (actually heroic) thing to do.

If it turns out the person was serious, you probably will have saved a life—or lives. In addition, you will have helped prevent the person making the threat from doing something completely regrettable—something that could negatively affect his or her life forever.

If it turns out the person making the threat was only kidding or making an idle threat, good. Nobody will have been hurt, and the person will learn not to make those kinds of jokes and threats.

Just like you can't make jokes at an airport about bombs and guns, you can't make jokes about guns and bombs at school.

Everybody understands that, or should.

# CHAPTER 6

# DANGER
## *Zones:*
## DRINKING, SMOKING, AND DOING DRUGS

## TOBACCO, ALCOHOL, AND OTHER DRUGS

Now that you're getting older, you may hear about or know kids who are experimenting with tobacco, alcohol, or drugs. Knowing the facts about these substances can help you avoid the problems associated with their use.

### *The Effects of Alcohol*

When a person drinks an alcoholic beverage, such as beer, wine, or hard liquor, the alcohol is absorbed into the bloodstream through the stomach and intestines. Since alcohol doesn't need to be broken down to be absorbed, like food, it enters the bloodstream quickly—within a few minutes.

Alcohol circulates throughout the body. It circulates through the brain, where it initially causes a sense of well-being. It can also cause feelings of great self-confidence, insight, and ability. In reality, though, alcohol diminishes ability: It dulls awareness, slows reflexes, impairs judgment, and interferes with physical coordination.

The more alcohol a person drinks, the more profound the effects are on the brain and other systems of the body. Drinking alcohol can cause a person to become confused, to stumble, to have slurred speech, to vomit, and to lose consciousness (pass out). Drinking too much alcohol can result in alcohol poisoning, which causes hundreds of deaths each year.

### Alcohol Poisoning

Drinking too much alcohol can become a medical emergency. Too much alcohol can cause the brain to stop giving out the signals that tell the lungs to breathe. Without oxygen, the heart cannot beat—and a person can die simply because he or she has drunk too much. Too much alcohol can cause someone to pass out or fail to wake up or be woken up. A person who has passed out may throw up while asleep and choke on the vomit. If you suspect alcohol poisoning or believe that a drunk person's safety is otherwise in jeopardy, call 911 (or another police emergency number) and ask for paramedics (an ambulance) to come. Don't worry about whether or not somebody will get into trouble because of underage drinking. Just get help!

### *Why do people drink, anyway?*

Adults who drink alcohol usually drink it to relax, often in a social setting. After having a few drinks, a person may become talkative or may "loosen up."

Although people may feel "high" while drinking, alcohol is a **depressant** (it slows the body's systems down). And many people experience feelings of "being down" after the initial effects of alcohol have worn off.

Responsible drinkers are aware of the effects that alcohol can have on their systems. They know their limits and stay within them. But drinking responsibly not only involves knowing how much to drink. It also involves knowing when, where, and with whom it is safe to drink. Managing the effects of alcohol can be tricky, and that's why the legal drinking age is 21.

## Impaired Judgment and Alcohol

A person who is under the influence of alcohol has impaired judgment. He or she may make bad decisions or take dangerous risks, like driving a car or riding with a drunk driver, or going off someplace with someone he or she doesn't know well enough to trust.

Because alcohol impairs judgment and reflexes, people should not swim, dive, water-ski, wakeboard, surf, wind-surf, body-surf, snow-ski, snowboard, skateboard, rock climb, or participate in any other sports or activities that are inherently dangerous while under the influence of alcohol.

Bad judgment can also come into play regarding sex. Alcohol affects people's moods. Under the influence of alcohol, people may have romantic feelings or sexual urges that they act on but normally wouldn't or shouldn't—and later regret. Also, they may decide to have sex without regard for the risk of pregnancy or the spread of sexually transmitted diseases. For example, HIV—which causes AIDS—is often spread when people who have been drinking take a chance and have sex without using a latex condom (see page 94).

A person under the influence of alcohol is an easy target for being harmed, because he or she is physically and emotionally vulnerable.

## Just refuse to go.

No exceptions: **Don't ride with a driver who's been drinking!** A person who has been drinking may reassure you that he or she can drive "just fine," but one of the effects of drinking alcohol is a false sense of confidence. The person cannot drive "just fine."

People under the influence of alcohol have impaired judgment and reflexes, which affect, among other things, how they react to sounds, to what they see, and to the speed of other vehicles. It causes drivers to operate vehicles recklessly, without regard to the safety of their passengers, other drivers, or themselves. People impaired by alcohol cause serious, often fatal, accidents with vehicles—cars, trucks, motorcycles, bicycles, and recreational vehicles, including boats, Jet Skis, and snowmobiles.

If a person who has been drinking offers to drive you somewhere, just don't go—and try to convince him or her not to drive. If you can get help from an adult, do. Hiding keys, calling a cab—even calling the police—are things people can do to prevent a drunk driver from going out onto the road.

## What if he or she has drunk just a little bit?

Alcohol interferes with reflexes and judgment long before a person is visibly drunk. A kid is not equipped to judge whether or not another person is okay to drive; call your parent or another responsible driver you trust if you find yourself in a situation in which an adult or teen who is in charge of your transportation has been drinking alcohol.

## Sobering Up

Taking a cold shower, drinking black coffee, or being walked around by a friend does NOT sober somebody up. The amount of time elapsed since the last drink, body weight, how many drinks have been consumed, and how much someone has eaten are the relevant factors affecting drunkenness and sobriety (the state of being sober).

## Experimenting with Alcohol

Underage drinkers don't always understand that experimenting with alcohol can involve more than just "seeing how it feels" to get drunk. Here are some of the risks that can be associated with youthful experimentation with alcohol:

1. Being killed or injured in a drunk-driving accident.
2. Getting alcohol poisoning.
3. Spontaneously trying drugs/overdosing on drugs.
4. Getting a sexually transmitted disease.
5. Being sexually molested/assaulted.
6. Getting into a fight and getting hurt/hurting somebody else (which may involve criminal charges).
7. Getting a girl pregnant.
8. Getting arrested for being a minor in possession of alcohol.
9. Getting arrested for being drunk in public.
10. Getting suspended or expelled from school.
11. Being denied a driver's license or having a driver's license suspended—whether or not a vehicle is involved.
12. Being charged with a crime related to drunk driving (example: vehicular homicide).

### HEADS UP!
**When mentally and physically impaired by alcohol, a drunk person is considered unable to make responsible decisions about sex. Even if the drunk person says yes, appears agreeable to the prospect of having sex, or initiates the sexual encounter, it doesn't count as consent (see page 125).**

**Having sex (or sexual contact) with a drunk person is wrong and may constitute "date rape" (or sexual assault). These are serious criminal offenses (see page 125).**

## TOBACCO

Tobacco can be used legally by anyone over age 18. It is available in the form of cigarettes and cigars; loose tobacco comes in packages for pipes or for rolling into cigarettes. Smokeless (chewing) tobacco comes in small cans.

It's relatively easy to get hooked on tobacco, but it's hard to quit. There's a substance present in tobacco called **nicotine**.

Nicotine is powerfully addictive. Once people have used tobacco for a while, they feel compelled to keep using it. During the course of the day, at intervals, a person gets a strong yearning for a cigarette. Reaching for a cigarette may also become an automatic response to certain situations that include feeling worried, upset, nervous, anxious, or excited.

Some people first try smoking cigarettes or chewing tobacco because they're curious and/or because their friends are trying it. They're also responding to tobacco ads, which are designed by the tobacco industry to interest nonsmokers in smoking.

Tobacco ads try to make people associate smoking with popularity, confidence, success, beauty, and—sex. For that reason, adolescents can be especially susceptible to the ads.

After smoking a cigarette, a smoker's mouth tastes and smells like cigarettes. Smoke lingers in clothing and hair. Tobacco stains teeth. Its long-term use can cause gum disease, which contributes to tooth loss and bad breath. How gross is that?

It seems that the tobacco industry would like us to forget that tobacco is linked with profound

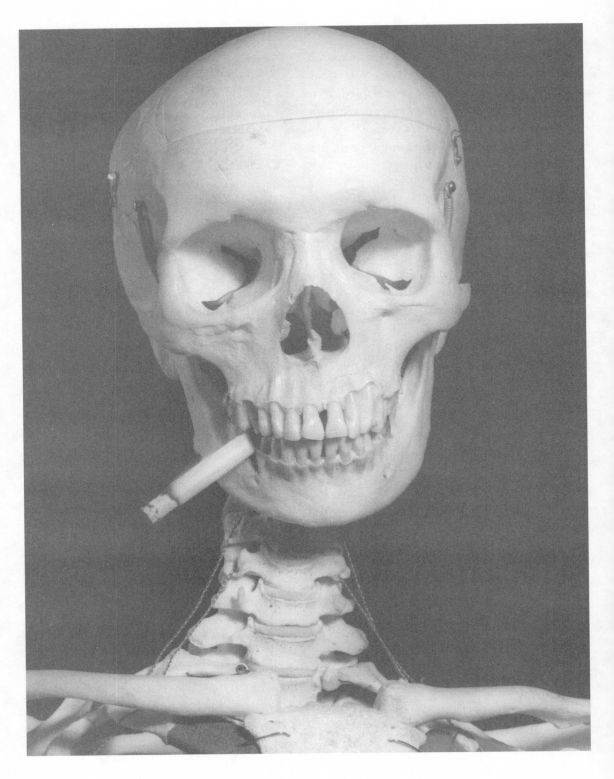

54

health problems, including cancer, heart disease, and respiratory illness, but 400,000 Americans die of tobacco-related illnesses every year.

This means that 400,000 fewer people will be buying cigarettes. The tobacco industry needs to recruit beginning smokers to replace them—like you, for example.

Many tobacco ads associate tobacco with fresh air and outdoor activity. They feature beautiful people having a great time while romping on the beach, hiking in the wilderness, wrangling cattle on the open range, skiing down snowy peaks.

What's *that* about? Smoking makes performing all of these activities more difficult, since it makes regular breathing more difficult.

## Drugs

A drug is a chemical substance. Used correctly, drugs can prevent, treat, control, or cure disease. Others help people manage pain. Drugs can treat mental conditions, such as depression, or physical conditions, such as hay fever.

1. Legal drugs (medicines) include **over-the-counter** drugs, such as ibuprofen, which anybody can buy, and **prescription** drugs, such as antibiotics, which a pharmacist fills according to a doctor's request.

2. Illegal drugs include substances such as heroin, cocaine, "speed," LSD, "ecstasy," and many others.

Sometimes legal drugs are used illegally—such as when a person uses a prescription drug for a different purpose from what was intended when it was prescribed.

## Taking Over-the-Counter Drugs

Over-the-counter drugs don't require a doctor's prescription, but they do require responsible, careful use. Ask your parents' permission before taking an over-the-counter drug, like a cough medicine, for example. Read the entire label, including the warnings, and check the recommended dose.

Don't take more than the recommended dose. Don't combine drugs without checking with the pharmacist or your doctor first. Combining drugs, including over-the-counter drugs, can be dangerous. So can drinking alcohol while taking drugs, including over-the-counter drugs.

> ➤ **Don't take, or give anyone, medicine in the dark or when you're sleepy. It's important to be alert when taking medicine.**
>
> **If you need medicine in the middle of the night, wake up a parent and ask for help getting out the correct medicine and taking it.**

## Taking Prescription Drugs

Containers that hold prescription drugs sometimes look alike. Before you take any prescription medicine, make sure that it has your name on it, that it's the right medicine, that you know the correct amount to take, and that you're taking it for the reason for which it was prescribed. And don't skip doses.

Your doctor should be aware of all medications you are taking before prescribing additional drugs.

## Remember

You can call the pharmacy and ask to talk to a pharmacist to make sure it's okay for drugs to be taken in combination with each other.

The call is free, and the pharmacist will be happy to give you this information.

## ILLEGAL DRUG USE

Heroin, crack cocaine, cocaine, "crank" (speed), LSD (acid), and "designer drugs" (such as "ecstasy") are examples of illegal drugs that are used by people who want to alter the way they feel.

### HEADS UP!

The "date-rape drug" is an illegal drug often used for criminal purposes. A person under the influence of the drug remains conscious but has no memory of events that transpire while drugged.

People have been raped, sexually assaulted, and robbed by others who have sneaked the date-rape drug into their drinks. Death from overdose has also occurred. In the future, if you go to parties, don't let someone you don't know get you or give you a drink. Get it yourself and don't leave it unattended. If you forget and do leave it unattended (for example, to dance or use the bathroom), dump it and get a new one.

Drugs may seem to provide a temporary escape from reality and responsibility, tension, anxiety (nervousness), or boredom. But the feelings that drugs produce are unpredictable and don't necessarily provide this escape. If they do provide it, it's just an illusion. The drug wears off, and the person experiences a letdown. Plus, the person's problems remain unresolved.

## If a drug is addictive . . .

The person will feel a compelling need to take the drug again. The impulse can be so strong that the person will take it even though he or she knows it's damaging.

Some people turn to crime, including prostitution (being paid to have sex), to get money to buy the drug to which they are addicted. So, many people end up in jail as a result of drug addiction!

Drugs can cause permanent damage to the vital organs of the body, including the brain. Certain drugs cause people to become violent, homicidal (murderous), or suicidal.

## Experimenting with Drugs

Teenagers may become curious about drugs and tempted to experiment. Just don't. Experimentation can lead to abuse, addiction, and emotional and physical harm. It can also lead to getting in trouble with the police.

The legal consequences of being caught in possession of illegal drugs are serious. Laws vary from state to state. Although some kids are ordered to attend drug education and rehab programs, not everybody is given this opportunity. It depends on the charges, the circumstances, and the type of drug use involved.

All people, including teens, are expected to know and follow laws—including laws involving alcohol and drugs. Kids who are caught possessing, using, and/or selling illegal drugs may end up spending a considerable amount of time in the juvenile hall, a youth-detention camp, or even jail if tried as an adult.

## Impaired Judgment and Drugs

Like alcohol, drugs can impair judgment and make people less likely to think about consequences and therefore less likely to protect themselves (and others) against dangerous situations, including exposure to HIV, the virus that causes AIDS (see page 87). HIV is often spread in situations where people decide to have sex while under the influence of drugs or alcohol.

## Different Kinds of Illegal Drugs

Some illegal drugs are swallowed, some are smoked, some are snorted up the nose. Others are injected into the body with needles (this is called "shooting up"). Shooting up drugs into a vein can lead to drug overdose and death. Sharing the needles and syringes used to shoot up drugs, including steroids, can spread HIV (see page 88) and other diseases.

**Stimulants** (uppers) make people feel "wired" or "fired up."

**Depressants** (downers) make people feel "slowed down."

**Hallucinogens** alter the perception of space and time and cause people to see and hear things that aren't real.

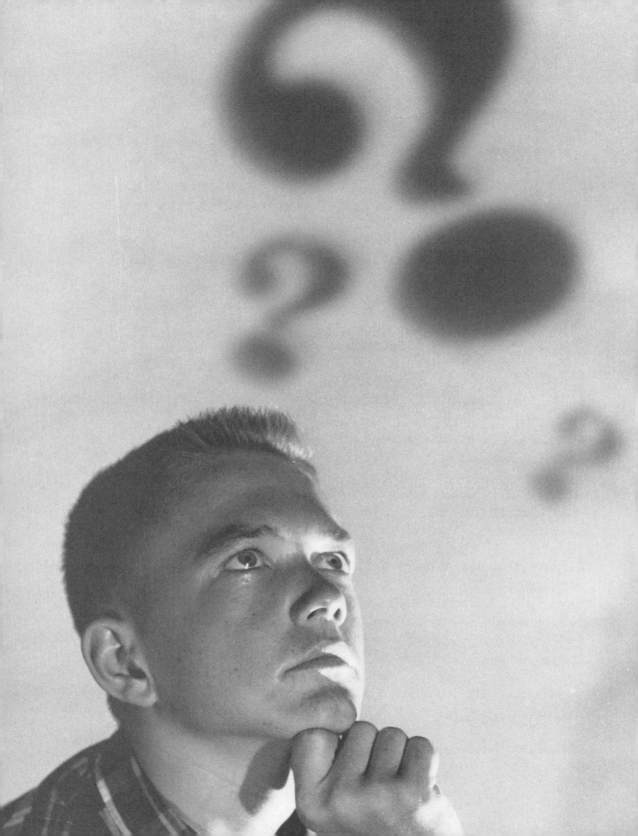

**Steroids** are used illegally by some people for the purpose of becoming more "buff" and/or improving their athletic performance. Abuse of steroids can cause dangerous mood swings, heart damage, sexual dysfunction, and other physical problems.

## Sniffing Chemical Inhalants (Huffing)

Many products that can be purchased legally, including household products, can be dangerous or deadly when misused. It's extremely risky and unhealthy to attempt to "get high" by inhaling the fumes of household products; in fact, it's reckless. Huffing can cause permanent brain damage, heart damage, liver damage, and death.

## Marijuana

Marijuana is a plant. Its dried leaves can be rolled up into a thin cigarette (sometimes called a "joint") and smoked. A few moments after the smoke is drawn into the lungs, it begins to take effect. Marijuana (also known as "weed" or "pot") is also sometimes eaten (after being baked into brownies, for example).

People who use marijuana do so because they like the way it makes them feel: Some feel relaxed; others believe it makes them think better; some just feel that it heightens their enjoyment of life. These feelings aren't consistent, though. Marijuana is also known to make people feel frightened, alienated, lonely, scared, or upset.

People have been arguing for years about whether marijuana is safe enough to be made legal. Regardless of these arguments, it is still absolutely against the law to use or be in possession of marijuana unless it has been legally prescribed by a physician for a valid medical reason under guidelines set by state and federal law—and even this is surrounded by controversy.

In any event, marijuana is still not considered a harmless substance. Marijuana smoke, like tobacco smoke, leaves a residue in the lungs. Also, it contains a mind-altering ingredient (THC). THC can cause psychological problems for some people who use it.

Like alcohol, marijuana can impair judgment. So, many of the problems associated with alcohol use apply to marijuana use—including the risks of driving while under the influence and of having sex while under the influence (and as a result: spreading or getting a sexually transmitted disease or causing an unplanned pregnancy).

## The Munchies

Marijuana can also make you want to eat, a response sometimes known as "having the munchies." The munchies can cause you to overeat and, in the long term, become overweight.

### FYI
Sometimes marijuana is "laced" with a more dangerous drug (heroin, for example), which has an unexpected, devastating effect on the person smoking it.

## Frequent use of marijuana by teens ...

Among other things, marijuana interferes with the natural development of coping skills. Teens who use marijuana may rely on it to escape the challenging feelings of everyday life, rather than experiencing the feelings and learning to deal with them.

Frequent use can cause bad grades, leading kids to drop out of school. That's because marijuana is known to interfere with motivation and concentration—two essential ingredients for being a successful student.

## Legal Considerations

At the time of the publication of this book, the use of marijuana for medical purposes, such as controlling nausea during chemotherapy (cancer treatment), is allowed in some areas, but this may change. Where permitted, a prescription written by a medical doctor under a certain (narrow) set of circumstances is required if the marijuana use is to be considered legal.

But every state has consequences for people caught possessing and/or using marijuana illegally. Since the use of marijuana is widespread, people sometimes "forget" about the legal consequences of getting caught, or they feel like it's no big deal to get caught. But it is a big deal!

There are places where possession of even the tiniest amount of marijuana, like one seed, for example, is a **felony** (very serious crime).

Even in states that are more lenient toward possession of a tiny amount (considering it a lesser crime: a misdemeanor), growing a marijuana plant may still be considered a felony. And it's always considered serious to *sell* marijuana.

### HEADS UP!
We *learn* to deal with stress, frustration, anxiety, and other uncomfortable feelings.

Those who use drugs to make the stressful feelings go away don't confront the feelings and don't develop good strategies for dealing with life's challenges.

As a result, teens who routinely use alcohol, marijuana, and other drugs can impair their development into strong and confident adults.

### Anyone who has a problem with drugs can get help.

It's completely possible to get help with a drug or alcohol problem without getting in trouble with the police. The National Council on Alcoholism and Drug Dependence Hope Line number (for the U.S. and Canada) is 1-800-NCA-CALL (1-800-622-2255).

The call is free and confidential and won't appear on the phone bill.

# CHAPTER 7

# SHARING THE ROAD: *Girls*

## STANDARD EQUIPMENT

Just like with guys, the onset of puberty causes changes in a girl's body that relate to her reproductive system: Her external and internal reproductive organs grow and change.

The physical changes in a girl's external reproductive organs (**vulva**) are pretty subtle, and except for growing pubic hair on the outside, she might not notice them. It's hard for a girl to see what's going on down there. In fact, it requires a mirror to get a good look.

### *Parts*

Like guys, girls have two gonads—called **ovaries.** And just like a guy's gonads, a girl's gonads have dual roles: They produce sex hormones (**estrogen** and **progesterone**) and they produce reproductive cells. Female reproductive cells are called **ova** (eggs). Each ovary produces just one tiny **ovum** (egg) every other month.

Eggs are produced in the ovaries at the same tem-

perature as the rest of the body, so it isn't necessary for a girl's gonads to hang down like a boy's do.

They are located inside her body, along with her **uterus** (womb), **fallopian tubes** (tubes that connect the ovaries to the womb), and **cervix** (bottom of the uterus). These make up her internal reproductive organs. The vulva includes the **mons**, the **outer lips**, the **inner lips**, and the **clitoris**, which is a small bump located at the top of the inner lips, where they come together. The **vagina** is the passage leading from the uterus to the vulva.

### *The Clitoris*

Like the penis, the clitoris has a glans and a shaft. It also has erectile tissue, which swells and gets harder when a girl is sexually aroused.

An erect clitoris is only about as big as a pea—but like a penis, it's capable of producing intense physical pleasure: an orgasm.

When a girl has an orgasm, she doesn't release reproductive cells, like a guy does.

A girl is born with all of the eggs she'll ever have; her body isn't capable of making new ones.

Her eggs mature just a few at a time, over a period of many days, and are released just one at a time, every other month. Each mature egg is released according to an inner clock, which is regulated by her hormones.

Unlike the penis, the clitoris doesn't play a role in the reproductive system. Females can produce children without any help from the clitoris. The sole purpose of the clitoris is to provide pleasure. It doesn't produce or distribute anything. But since it does produce intense sexual pleasure when stimulated, the clitoris provides an incentive for a female to have sexual contact with a male.

The size of the clitoris, like the size of a penis, varies a little, but not much. Every clitoris is small, and every one works. Girls don't worry one bit about the size.

Just below the clitoris is the opening that a girl pees out of, her **urethra**, which is *not* part of her reproductive system. Below that is the vaginal opening, which leads into the vagina.

### The Vagina

The vagina is like a soft, warm, moist passageway. Its opening is sometimes, but not always, covered by a fold of membrane called the **hymen**. The vagina plays a key role in the reproductive process. For one thing, it's the passageway through which a baby is born.

How can a baby come out of such a small opening? The walls of the vagina are stretchy. Nevertheless, it's a very tight squeeze.

The vagina has another role: to receive the sperm that the penis distributes.

The act of placing an erect penis into the vagina of a female and ejaculating is called having **sexual intercourse**. Sexual intercourse is described in detail on page 72. But briefly, what happens is this:

During sexual intercourse, about 6 million sperm are dispatched by the penis inside of a female's vagina. One lucky sperm may find the egg and get inside it, triggering a response that shuts all the other sperm out — kind of like slamming the door in their faces. A sperm uniting with an egg marks the beginning of a sequence of events that leads to a baby being born.

## CONTROL PANELS: HORMONES

Hormones are secreted by various organs in a girl's body — just like they are in a boy's. Two key organs that produce hormones in a girl's body are her ovaries, which produce sex hormones.

Sex hormones are responsible for the regulation of the reproductive system and the changes a girl's body goes through during puberty. The two main girl hormones are **estrogen** and **progesterone**, and these basically run the show.

## Girls are growing breasts.

One of the first, most obvious, changes that happen to a girl at the onset of puberty is that she begins to grow breasts.

Breasts are considered accessory reproductive organs.

A girl's body grows breasts to prepare her for the possibility of breast-feeding, in case she decides to have a baby once she becomes physically mature. But breasts have another function: They're capable of producing pleasant sexual feelings when touched.

The first signs that breasts are developing are that nipples become larger and the area around the nipple (**areola**) gets wider. Then the nipple and areola darken. A small bump, called a **breast bud**, appears behind each nipple. Breast buds can appear as early as age 8, but they are more likely to appear at around age 10 or 11.

Inside of her breasts, a girl's milk-producing organs (**alveoli** and **milk ducts**) are growing. Around these, a layer of fat tissue develops—to protect them.

Breasts come in a variety of shapes and shades. They can be big or small, round or flat, dark or light. Nipple color relates to skin tone. Nipples can be brown, plum-colored, dark pink, or pale pink. Breasts aren't always symmetrical (perfectly matched). It's very common for one breast to be a little bigger than the other one.

Big or small, breasts are famous for capturing the attention of males; most guys really like looking at them (and touching them, when permitted).

### ➤ Breast Etiquette for Guys

Commenting—complimenting a girl on her breasts—is offensive. Example: "Nice rack."

Criticizing breasts is also unacceptable. Example: "How flat is *she*!"

Even if a guy is being complimentary or just kidding around, remarks made that relate to sexual characteristics (including breasts and breast development) are embarrassing, unwelcome, and just plain inappropriate.

They're also considered a kind of sexual *harassment* (see page 123).

## OGLING

Some boys feel like they can barely take their eyes off of a girl's breasts. During a conversation, it's sometimes hard not to look down. It's helpful to look into a girl's eyes or at her mouth when she's talking. Stay focused on the conversation.

Opportunities present themselves for a guy to subtly catch a glimpse without being obvious about it, and a quick glance shouldn't cause a problem. But don't stare! Girls are really tuned into guys checking them out. And girls can be just as self-conscious about their changing bodies as boys are about theirs, or more!

### Objectification

Separating someone's body from who she or he is as a person has a name: objectification. Who wants to be scrutinized as an object? Nobody. Girls hate this!

### "High Beams"

When a girl gets chilly, her nipples contract and become harder and poke out. Erect nipples can become pretty apparent under a girl's shirt. They may draw your eyes to her chest. Boys can't help but note this temporary, intriguing condition—but remember: A quick glance is all you get. Don't stare.

### Hugs

When you casually hug a girl, you'll feel her breasts pressing against your chest for a minute. This contact is part of every friendly hug—and you won't be cited for it.

The same goes for when you're slow dancing: It's part of the dance.

# CLASSIFIED INFORMATION

## ✔ About Bras

Girls usually feel more comfortable when their breasts are held snugly against their chests, especially when they jog, dance, or play sports. It's uncomfortable when breasts move around too much.

A bra provides support. A bra also provides a degree of privacy. It helps keep a girl's nipples from showing when she's wearing a thin shirt.

Some girls go braless (there's no law that says you've got to wear one). Others wear a tank top or a T-shirt under their clothes instead of a bra.

There are all kinds of bras—practical and fancy. Some hook in the back, some hook in the front. Some are strapless. Some are long—down to the waist (called "merry-widow bras" or "bustiers," à la Madonna).

Some are made from delicate material—very skimpy and flimsy. Not for soccer wear! Sports bras are made of thick, stretchy material. These really get the job done.

Bras aren't worn while sleeping.

## ✔ A cup, B cup—what's that about?

Most bras have a letter and a number for a size—like 36A, for example. The number relates to the measurement around the chest, below the breasts. The letter corresponds to the size of the breast itself. Cup sizes, from smallest to biggest, are AAA, AA, A, B, C, D, DD, and DD/E.

## ✔ Additional Random Bra Info

Nursing bras have flaps over the nipples that unhook and drop down so a baby can drink.

Padded bras? The name explains them. They're bras with padding inside—to make breasts look bigger. **Miracle Bras** and **Wonderbras** are two examples. These are craftily constructed with padding so that breasts are uplifted and pushed closer together, creating an illusion of cleavage (the "valley" where two breasts meet).

Some fashions don't allow for a bra (like backless formal dresses, for example). Girls can wear "stick-on bras" with backless dresses. These are basically two separate bra "cups" with adhesive around the edges. They work fairly well, except they're kind of uncomfortable to peel off.

But if a boy actually tries to feel a girl's breasts by rubbing his chest against her, it's different. The hug will have gone from friendly to sexual, and this will be totally obvious to the girl.

Will she like it?

Under most circumstances, no.

### The girls are getting furrier.

Like guys, girls grow more hair on their bodies during puberty: pubic hair, underarm hair, hair on their legs.

This new hair grows to a certain length (short) and then stops, on both boys and girls. It doesn't keep on getting longer, like the hair on our heads. When shaved off, it grows right back in—like whiskers do on a guy.

Pubic hair, when fully grown in, looks like an upside-down triangle on a girl's body. It can be curly or straight, brown, black, red, or blond.

Occasionally, some girls style it—by trimming it a little bit.

Sometimes girls shave off some of their pubic hair so it won't peek out of a bathing suit. That's called the "bikini line."

The bikini line can also be adjusted by "waxing"—which essentially pulls the hairs out. Ouch? You're right.

Not all girls care about trimming, shaving, or waxing the bikini line. Or de-fuzzing legs or armpits, for that matter.

Neither does every guy. A lot of guys couldn't care less if girls have hair on their legs and under their arms—in fact, they like it.

> ➤ De-fuzzing, Girl-Style . . .
> Girls who shave their legs and armpits usually use a safety razor. They usually just shave between the ankle and the knee (not the kneecap) and under both arms. Stray hairs higher up on the fronts and backs of the legs (thighs) may also be policed.
> A few girls shave with an electric shaver—

not many, though. Some may wax their legs.

Some girls use hair-removing products. These are smeared on and rinsed off a few minutes later—after the hair has been dissolved by chemicals.

### New sweat glands are beginning to work.

During puberty, the girls are sweating more. And like many boys, many girls are beginning to use deodorant/antiperspirant.

### They're growing taller and gaining weight.

Girls also have a growth spurt during puberty, and it generally occurs earlier in the female's sequence of changes than it does in the male's.

That's why so many of the girls in middle school and junior high are taller and bigger than the boys are. Eventually the boys catch up and surpass the girls in size and strength. This is because the growth spurt of males lasts longer than the growth spurt of females.

A girl's growth spurt isn't only about height. Gaining fat is a normal, necessary part of female development.

### Soft to the Touch

Girls get round during puberty. Fat tissue increases as part of breast development. A girl's hips increase in size and change in shape, and so do her thighs.

This increase in fat tissue is partly in anticipation of bearing children, when women need to have reserves of energy, which can be stored in fat.

### Their skin is getting oilier.

They may be developing acne on the face, shoulders, and back.

## The Main Event

They're starting their periods (or **menstruating**).

When a girl's period starts, it's major—comparable to when a boy ejaculates for the first time. Beginning to have periods means that her eggs have begun to mature. **Ovulation** may begin anytime during the next 2 years and occur unpredictably during that time.

Once a girl begins to ovulate regularly, her periods may become more regular as well. The cycle is controlled by hormonal activity and will repeat itself until she's about 50.

A girl's period usually begins when she's about 13—but it can happen at any time between the ages of 9 and 16.

When she's having a period, which lasts a few days, a small amount of bloody fluid trickles out of a girl's body via her vagina. But the girl isn't actually bleeding from an injury. Just a certain predetermined amount of blood is being released.

Then it stops.

And then the cycle starts all over again.

Once it starts, most girls have a period once a month. It takes a while for a girl's reproductive system to get into the rhythm of having a period regularly. Regularly means according to a routine schedule—for example, every 28 days. Not all girls have regular periods, but most do.

## Q. AND A.

**Q. Where does the blood come out?**
**A.** It comes out of the vaginal opening.

**Q. Where does the blood come from?**
**A.** It originates in the uterus (womb)—a small, expandable, pear-shaped organ. It's located inside of a girl's body, about halfway between her belly button and her crotch.

When a woman becomes pregnant, the baby grows in the uterus—not in the stomach, which is an organ that both males and females have for digesting food.

**Q. Why does blood come out?**
**A.** Once a girl goes through puberty, her uterus makes a special lining of bloody tissue every month to prepare for a possible pregnancy. If a pregnancy were to occur, the lining would nourish the **embryo** as it grew and developed inside the uterus. (An embryo is a group of cells that develops into a **fetus**, which is the beginnings of a baby.)

If a pregnancy doesn't occur, the lining of the uterus isn't needed to nourish an embryo, and so the lining is released (as menstrual fluid). Releasing this fluid once a month is what having a period is all about.

Girls and women don't have periods during the months that they are pregnant.

That's why missing a period is usually the very first sign of pregnancy (see page 73).

Once pregnancy has occurred, the lining of the uterus isn't shed; instead, it becomes an organ called the **placenta**.

The placenta provides nourishment to the developing fetus. It acts as a filter between the mother and the fetus, keeping their blood separated. It allows nutrients and dissolved oxygen to enter the fetus's bloodstream. It eliminates waste. But the placenta is *not* a perfect filter. If the mom does drugs, drinks alcohol, or smokes, the fetus can be harmed.

The placenta is expelled from the uterus just after the baby is born.

**Q. How does the blood get from the uterus into the vagina?**
**A.** The cervix is the bottom of the uterus. The blood comes out of a small hole in the cervix. The hole, called the **os**, opens into the vagina.

**Q. What does having a period *feel* like?**

**A.** It feels like leaking a little bit of liquid. The leaking can't be controlled, like when people urinate (pee). It just comes out—whenever.

**Q. Does having a period *hurt*?**
**A.** Sometimes it involves having a big, fat, dull ache (**cramps**) in the abdomen or lower back, especially during the first day or two.

Girls can take over-the-counter or prescription medicine, lie in a comfortable position with a warm hot-water bottle on the abdomen—or even exercise to relieve cramps.

**Q. Pads—what's with those?**
**A.** Girls can wear throwaway pads (soft, absorbent ones) in their underwear during the days they are menstruating. The pads have sticky stuff on the back so that they stay in place (stuck to the underwear, not to the girl).

They are changed every few hours, or sooner if necessary.

**Q. How does a girl know when she's going to start her period for the first time?**
**A.** It's always a surprise. But at least she gets some clues: A girl won't start her period until she begins to grow breasts and also has quite a bit of pubic hair.

One day or night, she'll notice a smudge, stain, or dribble of blood in her underwear and . . . ta-da! Her period will have arrived. For some girls, this is cause for a great celebration. For others, it's a giant pain in the neck.

Sooner or later, though, everybody gets used to it.

**Q. If a girl doesn't have a pad—then what?**
**A.** For emergency purposes, she can use a wad of toilet paper, a stack of tissues, a folded-up paper towel, a clean washcloth—or even a clean sock.

A lot of girls and women carry pads in their purse or backpack and are happy to give one away if someone is in a pinch.

The school nurse and/or office manager almost always has a stash of pads for girls who start during the school day.

You may see blood on the back of a girl's clothes, and if you do, be cool. Don't put it on the ten o'clock news.

## Pad Wrangling

Should you ever be asked to hook up your mom, your sister, or another female with pads, hey—you can do it! And it will really be appreciated.

Pads can be easily found in grocery stores, drugstores, and convenience stores. There's a sea of choices. Unless you have been given other instructions, any brand of pad that says "maxi" on it is a safe choice.

Don't choose "panty liners."

Tampons are not pads; if you've been dispatched for pads, don't bring back tampons, which are sold in the same area as pads.

### James's Old Trick

Once upon a time, a long time ago, my friend started her period for the very first time when she was visiting her grandma and grandpa out in the country.

Her grandma wasn't home, so her grandpa volunteered to walk to the local store. An old trick when buying pads is to buy something else at the same time. That way the focus isn't so much on the pads. So her grandpa craftily selected a small box of Ex-Lax (poop medicine) for himself. Then he picked up a large box of pads and casually put both items on the counter.

The owner of the store, an old friend of his, stared at the Ex-Lax and at the box of pads. Then he leaned real close and said, "James? Are you all right?"

James was fine.

And so will all the other brave guys be fine who get dispatched to snag pads for sisters, friends, girlfriends, moms, grandmas. Or apparently, granddaughters.

**Q. Not pads? Then what are they?**

**A.** A lot of girls use tampons instead of pads. A tampon is carefully poked up into the vagina, where it absorbs menstrual blood before the blood leaves the body. Most tampons have a cardboard or plastic applicator, which helps the girl direct the tampon into place.

Like pads, tampons fill up with blood and must be changed regularly.

There is a string incorporated into a tampon for pulling it out. Tampons are either flushed or wrapped and tossed into the trash.

Tampons must be used responsibly because if used incorrectly, they can pose a health risk. That's why there are instructions on every box of tampons, and girls are encouraged to read and follow them carefully.

**Q. PMS—what's up with that?**

**A.** Hormone fluctuations during the course of each menstrual cycle can cause mood changes.

"PMS" stands for **premenstrual syndrome**, and, among other things, it's about feeling grouchy before a period. It can also be about puffiness in the hands, face, and abdomen and having tender breasts.

PMS can include general irritability, door slamming, toothbrush throwing, arguments with friends and family, and fits of sobbing over things like greeting-card commercials.

It may account for the times your mom, step-mom, or foster mom loses it—just because every article of clothing you own has been thrown on your bedroom floor, along with your bicycle helmet, snowboarding goggles, fish food, and clarinet.

➤ **Gr-r-r-r-r-r!**
Mentioning PMS, especially when somebody has symptoms of PMS, is extraordinarily risky.
If you suspect PMS, it's safest to say nothing.

It is so infuriating when somebody else brings up the topic, especially if it's a guy.

It's obnoxious to make PMS comments. Girls won't think it's funny because it's not!

PMS can go beyond grouchiness and/or weepiness.

It can be a source of serious physical and emotional upsets, and a number of girls and women have to alter their diets, take medication, and otherwise seek the help of health care professionals to establish a treatment plan for relieving the symptoms of premenstrual stress.

## It lasts how long?!

Women have periods until about age 50. Then they stop. This is called menopause. After menopause, women are no longer able to conceive children. Their ovaries don't produce any more eggs.

Menopause has wide-ranging effects—the most famous of which are hot flashes, when a woman feels boiling hot for no reason. Do you have a 50-something woman in your family who randomly gripes about being hot?

So now ya know.

## Handsome Knight in Hooded Sweatshirt

I'll admit it. As far as a boy-meets-girl story goes, this is an unusual one:

When my friend was in college, she unexpectedly started her period while in class—and didn't realize it until she stood up to leave.

A cute guy, a student, walked up to her and said, "I've got five sisters. Want to tie this around your waist?"

He took off his sweatshirt and handed it to her.

She tied his sweatshirt around her waist, and he walked her to her dorm.

After that, they figured out that they liked each other and started dating.

The moral of the story is: Be a cool guy—you never know what may happen as a result.

## Girls are getting stronger sexual feelings.

Girls, like boys, experience a wide range of feelings during puberty because puberty has profound physical and emotional effects.

Girls get crushes, just like boys.

Many fantasize about sexual situations.

And many girls, like most boys, masturbate.

A girl masturbates by (gently) stimulating her clitoris. As she becomes more and more sexually aroused, her sex organs go through subtle physical changes (swell, change color). Her heart rate increases; her rate of breathing gets faster. If she has an orgasm, it will be of the same intensity as a male's. Unlike most males, a female can have several orgasms in a row without waiting for time to pass in between.

Fewer girls than boys masturbate because masturbating is a little harder to figure out for girls than it is for boys.

A boy's penis is pretty obvious; he can't miss it. And he routinely has occasion to touch it.

But a girl's clitoris is small and well hidden—in a place she doesn't pay much attention to, unless she's hunting for it.

Some girls don't even know they have one!

A girl can have an orgasm in her sleep, but since she doesn't ejaculate, wetting her sheets or pajamas isn't an issue.

She usually just wakes up momentarily and then falls back asleep—with the hopes of having the same dream again!

Z-Z-Z-Z-Z-Z-z-z-z-z-z-z-z-z-z-z-z-z-z-z . . .

# CHAPTER 8

# THE (RE)PRODUCTION LINE:
# SEXUAL
## *Reproduction*

To reproduce means to make anew; it means to make again. No species could continue to inhabit the earth without having the ability to reproduce.

All living creatures reproduce, from the tiniest moth to the hugest rhinoceros. But only some of them reproduce sexually.

When creatures reproduce sexually, it means that the male and the female parent each contributes genes to the offspring. Genes carry the information needed to form new life. They are contained in a female's egg and in the reproductive cells of a male and are united during the mating process.

### *Woof!*

How does sexual intercourse between people relate to cocker spaniels?

Thankfully, it doesn't.

Neither does it really relate to birds, bees, and other creatures in the animal kingdom.

In the animal kingdom, two male hoofed animals paw the ground, charge each other, bash heads, and lock antlers until one gives up. The winner then briefly mounts a female, who's somewhere nearby flicking her tail. Afterward, he thunders off in a cloud of dust and disappears into the bushes, never to be seen or heard of again.

## "THE TALK": GUY REPORT ON MAKING BABIES

"I first began learning about how people make babies from a children's book my parents gave me. I don't remember the title, but on the light green cover there was a picture of a boy and a cocker spaniel puppy. Inside the book were many stories about animals and animal babies and then a little section on people and human babies. The mechanics of reproduction were not described, but I got the idea that babies came from a mother and a father acting together in some way so the baby would start to grow and then be hatched.

"I never asked my parents about human reproduction. I got the feeling that this book with the boy and his puppy was about as far as they were willing to go."

# WE DON'T JUST MATE
## *Sexual Intercourse*

The following is an actual explanation of the act of people having (vaginal) sexual intercourse ("making love," "having sex"). Also explained is how sexual intercourse between human beings is related to making babies.

Under most circumstances, a woman, like a man, becomes sexually aroused during the activities that precede the act of intercourse (called foreplay). Foreplay can include making out, or going further and undressing together (see page 82).

When a woman is sexually aroused, slippery secretions are produced by the walls of her vagina and also by the membranes close to the entrance to her vagina. This makes it easier for the man's penis to enter.

During intercourse, the man's erect penis is placed in the woman's vagina. It becomes stimulated by the walls of her vagina as he moves it in and out and eventually ejaculates (and has an orgasm).

In the meantime, the woman's clitoris swells and gets erect. It withdraws under a hood of skin. During the act of sexual intercourse, the guy's penis tugs and rubs against the hood of skin, which indirectly stimulates the clitoris by friction.

This may or may not cause her to have an orgasm.

Having sexual intercourse is usually accompanied by strong, pleasurable emotional and physical sensations for both partners.

## *Adjusting the Timing*

When people become sexual partners, they can teach each other what feels good so that the experience of having sex together is satisfying for both. Usually, it takes practice for both to have an orgasm.

Since the clitoris is stimulated only indirectly

during intercourse, an orgasm for some women may be more likely to happen during foreplay or afterplay (after intercourse).

## How Pregnancy Happens

During intercourse, several million sperm zoom (well, wriggle, actually) through a tiny doorway called the **os** in the very bottom part of the uterus (cervix).

The sperm are basically on an egg hunt, and the odds of finding it first are 6 million to one!

Each sperm charges forward by lashing its tail tadpole-style. Millions frantically scout around in the uterus, where they will have absolutely no luck.

Some of the best navigators find their way up into the two fallopian tubes, which are attached to the uterus. In one of these two tubes, one tiny egg may be waiting. One (and only one) sperm will enter it. At this point, conception has taken place—the egg has been fertilized. The rest of the sperm will hang around, dying within a few days.

## Genes . . .

Contain genetic information and are present in both the sperm and the egg. Once united, the genes combine to provide the plan for a totally new and unique human being.

## Fertilized Egg

As soon as an egg is fertilized, it begins to grow by the process of cell division.

The fertilized egg (at first, one cell) divides. Then it divides again. And again. This process continues as the egg moves down the fallopian tube and into the uterus, where it will plant itself in the lining of the uterine wall.

After it is in place, its outer cells organize to form the **placenta**. The placenta surrounds the fertilized egg (now called an **embryo**) and grows along with it.

The placenta produces a hormone that causes changes in the mother's body that are needed to support a pregnancy. These changes include further development of the placenta and uterus, changes in the milk-producing glands in preparation for breast-feeding after the infant is born, and other changes that maintain a healthy environment as the embryo continues to grow.

## First Stage

In the first few weeks of the development of an embryo, the basic systems of the body are formed. When the embryo's body structures are in recognizable human shape (at 8 weeks), it is called a

**fetus**. The placenta provides nourishment for the developing fetus and eliminates its waste products. It also acts as a filter between the mother and the fetus, keeping their blood separated. It allows nutrients and dissolved oxygen to enter the fetus's bloodstream. The fetus is attached to the placenta by the **umbilical cord**. Its life is entirely supported by the mother's body.

The placenta is not a perfect filter. It is unable to filter out drugs or alcohol if they are present in the mother's bloodstream. So, to protect her developing fetus from harm, a pregnant woman should not smoke, drink alcohol, or take any drugs, unless prescribed by her doctor.

After 9 months have passed, the baby is ready to be born.

Nobody knows what triggers the onset of a baby's passage from a mother's uterus into the outside world (called "labor and delivery"). But when the time comes, the muscles of the uterus begin to contract, and these contractions cause the os in the cervix to open wider and wider. Once it is all the way open, it becomes time for the mother to push (bear down) as hard as she can with her belly muscles along with each contraction.

The baby's head stretches the walls of the vagina and makes way for the rest of the baby's body to fit out of the vaginal opening. The process of labor usually takes between 8 and 26 hours for a first baby, but the "pushing out" and delivery happens relatively quickly at the end of the labor.

The baby is born. It cries out and breathes. Its umbilical cord is cut.

The placenta is expelled shortly afterward.

A baby will have a belly button where the umbilical cord was once attached.

➤ Often, the father of the child is present to provide support, encouragement, and physical assistance to the mom as she is giving birth. Dads can provide a lot of help to moms during childbirth.

The thought of a woman pushing a baby out of her vagina may be a frightening image for some dads. But most discover that, since giving birth is usually a very long process, there is time to adjust to the situation.

Participating in the birth of a child can be an extremely profound experience for a dad; not only can he help the mom, he can be present to hold, reassure, and help care for his newborn baby.

## Alternative Insemination

Not all kids are conceived through sexual intercourse. Many are conceived through **alternative insemination** (or "donor insemination").

What happens is this:

A woman, usually in the office of a health care professional, receives sperm that has previously been collected from a male (through masturbating). The sperm is introduced into her vagina. If all goes well, the woman becomes pregnant.

In a more complicated medical procedure, a woman's egg(s) are **harvested** (removed) and mixed with sperm outside of her body. Later, the developing egg or eggs are introduced into her uterus, where they continue to grow.

All methods of human reproduction require both female and male reproductive cells—so it takes a guy's participation, no matter what.

Every birth is the result of the miraculous process of human reproduction, and every child is a natural wonder, regardless of whether conception of the baby takes place through intercourse or through an alternative method.

# CHAPTER 9

# *Parking:* SEX

Biologically speaking, sex is the compelling force behind human reproduction (see page 70). But sex isn't only about reproduction. If it were, couples would have only very specific sexual contact, and they'd only have it when they wanted to make a baby—and that's generally not how it works.

Unless actually planning a pregnancy, most couples intentionally avoid the link between sex and reproduction by stopping short of having sexual intercourse or by using birth control during sexual intercourse.

What is sexual intercourse? It's a kind of sexual activity that can lead to a woman's becoming pregnant. It's described on page 72.

Even though having sexual intercourse is sometimes called "having sex," and sex can be described as the compelling force behind human reproduction, sexual activity isn't necessarily a push toward sexual intercourse.

Far from it!

Sex is about exploring a whole range of sensations that feel good physically and emotionally, either with a partner or alone. And there are a variety of activities that go along with that.

Our sexuality develops as we grow from infancy into adulthood. And our awareness of sexual feelings often begins in infancy or early childhood, when we discover that touching our own bodies in certain ways feels good (see page 15).

## SEX AND LOVE

Being in love is about having a profoundly tender, passionate affection for another person. Sharing sexual feelings can be a way of expressing that affection. Having sexual contact with a partner is a way of communicating feelings through touching.

Not all couples include sex in their relationship. Some choose not to. Couples can find many ways to express love without having sex.

Many people consider sex to be an expression so special and intimate that it should be reserved for partners who are married or otherwise committed to a long-term, mutually faithful relationship based on love and trust.

Some adults have sexual relationships with consenting adult friends or adult acquaintances—without being in love. But for most people, sex and love are linked.

When linked with love, sex can be one of the

most powerful, intense, and satisfying experiences two people can share.

## However . . .

Sex, even when linked with love, isn't always powerful.

It would be unrealistic to think that every time two people have sex, the earth moves beneath them. More often, sex could be described as a comforting, reassuring experience that allows two people to snuggle up and touch bases with each other.

And sometimes (especially between inexperienced partners), sex can be downright disappointing!

## Crushes

A strong physical attraction can easily translate into a crush, and the feelings associated with having a crush can be really intense.

Is having a crush the same as falling in love? Not really.

Having a strong physical attraction to another person is one of the components of being in love, but being in love involves other feelings, too.

A crush can be on somebody you hardly know; a crush can even be on somebody you've never even talked to.

Being in love is about being connected to another person in the deepest, most profound way imaginable. Actually knowing the person is an essential ingredient of being in love.

Unbelievably (and *totally* unbelievably if you're in the middle of having a crush), crushes can fade relatively quickly and often do.

Even so, having a crush can cause some emotional havoc, especially when you're young, because even though a crush isn't love, it can feel like the real thing!

## Kids and Love (and Sex)

Sometimes kids do fall in love with each other. It may start with one or the other having a crush, with both people having a crush on each other, or with a friendship that moves in a romantic direction.

However it starts, it progresses into a situation where both people are extremely attracted to each other and acknowledge it. The feelings they share develop and deepen into a relationship that could be characterized as love.

## Even so . . .

Most teens lack the experience needed to fully accept the responsibilities and assume the risks that go along with having sex with a partner.

The responsibilities that go along with having a sexual relationship include making and keeping appointments for routine medical exams for the screening of sexually transmitted diseases, as well as knowing how to reduce the risks of being exposed to, or exposing someone else to, sexually transmitted diseases. This is true of both heterosexual and homosexual couples (see page 80). With heterosexual couples, responsibilities also include knowing how to take precautions to avoid unplanned pregnancy and how to act responsibly should an unplanned pregnancy occur.

But the risks of having sex aren't limited to physical risks; there are also emotional risks. Preadolescents and young teens are not yet equipped to cope with the complex set of emotions that accompany a sexual relationship.

➤ Apart from the moral and ethical issues that accompany having put a baby on the planet, do you know that a male may be held financially responsible for the baby he produces until the baby grows up and reaches the age of eighteen?

This can apply even if the father had no intent to become a dad or to have a long-term relationship with the mother of the child and even if the guy himself used birth control (a condom) and/or believed the mother of the child was using birth control effectively while having sex (see page 93).

It can apply even if the guy wanted the girl to have an abortion (see page 102) rather than go through with the pregnancy and even if he offered to pay for the abortion and she declined his offer.

## Peer Pressure About Sex

If you don't want to have sexual contact with a partner, don't. You don't have to give a reason—you don't even need to have a reason. You certainly don't have to have sex to prove your masculinity or to prove your affection for your partner.

There are lots of ways to show love that don't involve having sex.

Don't pressure yourself.

Peer pressure, when it comes right down to it, is really mostly about how we pressure ourselves. Most kids don't hound each other to have sex, smoke cigarettes, drink alcohol, or take drugs. Honor and respect your own ideas and instincts about what seems right for you.

Having a sexual relationship with somebody is a huge responsibility. If you don't feel ready to take it on, you're not ready—so don't.

You don't have to prove to yourself that you are capable of having sex.

"Being like the other guys" isn't a good reason to have sex—especially when you consider how many of the other boys are either exaggerating or just flat-out, full-on lying about it!

## You'll Know When

Once grown and fully mature, you'll be aware of and ready and able to accept the risks and responsibilities involved in having sex with a partner.

You'll be able to recognize when the situation is right. You'll be able to make the commitment required.

You'll be able to responsibly have sex with someone you love and trust, who loves and trusts you, too.

## Sex and the Media/Sex and the Myths

In our culture, sex is used to sell everything from toothpaste to chain saws. It's used to sell movie tickets, CDs, TV programs, magazines, and newspapers.

Since sexual images are used for the rather unimportant purpose of selling stuff to people, there's an unspoken message that sex is, well, not really all that special—but it is!

The media seem unrelenting in pressuring youth to have sex—and to be sexy. Young teens are bombarded by sexual images without being given enough actual information about sex and the risks and responsibilities associated with it. Kids are given the idea that "everybody" is doing it, or should be. They are also given the impression that adolescents are supposed to be sexy to be powerful and popular.

This may be part of the reason that so many boys feel pressured to have sex, even before they're ready to. But there's another reason: There is a societal myth that a guy has to have sex with a lot of girls (or even just one!) to prove that he's a man. Many boys exaggerate or just plain make up stories about sexual escapades to impress the other guys, and this just adds to the confusion.

Having sex doesn't make a boy a man—it just makes him a boy who's had sex. And if he just does it to get a feather in his cap—to impress his friends or to prove something to himself—where does the girl fit into the picture?

There's no good reason to rush into having sex, but there are a whole lot of good reasons not to.

Sexually transmitted diseases and unplanned pregnancy are only two of the reasons not to.

Sex can also put kids at risk of emotional harm if they're not actually ready for the experience.

> ➤ ~~Horse~~Studpower
> At a time when people are particularly attuned to the health risks involved with having multiple sexual partners, boasting about sexual conquests isn't likely to get a guy high marks.
>
> Being a stud is important if you're a retired racehorse, a prize bull, or a blue-ribbon hog. Apart from that, it has no particular credibility.

# SEXUAL ORIENTATION

The words **sexual orientation** describe whether a person is attracted to people of the opposite sex, people of the same sex, or people of both sexes. The concept of how people get their sexual orientation is not fully understood.

Some people believe that our sexual orientation is something that we are born with. Others feel that it develops as a result of our experiences. Many feel that our sexual orientation is a result of a combination of both these factors.

Sexual orientation is sometimes thought of in terms of categories: **heterosexual** (when all or most of a person's attractions are directed toward someone of the opposite sex); **homosexual** (when all or most of a person's attractions are directed toward someone of the same sex); or **bisexual** (when someone has attractions toward people of both sexes).

Here are words you may hear describing sexual orientation: **straight** (men who romantically love women and women who romantically love men); **gay** (men who romantically love men); **lesbian** (women who romantically love women); and **bi** (men or women who romantically love both men and women).

All are natural ways of being.

Many people reject the notion of putting people into categories and labeling them. Not everybody believes that people fit into one category or another. In any event, the groupings don't apply to kids, who are in the process of developing in all ways—including sexually.

Liking to hold hands, hug, and snuggle with friends of the same sex or of the opposite sex, or both, is common among young children. Sometimes sexual feelings accompany these affectionate gestures. These feelings don't necessarily predict what a person's sexual orientation will ultimately be.

Having a few "gay" or "lesbian" romantic attractions as a young teen also doesn't necessarily mean that the teen will grow up to be gay or lesbian.

But it might.

## *Don't fix what ain't broke.*

Homosexuality is a natural expression of human sexuality that has existed since the beginning of time. It's described by psychologists as a normal variation of human sexuality.

It's not regarded as a condition that needs to be treated, modified, medicated, changed, or fixed.

Understanding sexual orientation is the first step toward establishing healthy attitudes toward ourselves and others.

People can be strong, productive, respected, confident, healthy—and happy—regardless of sexual orientation.

## *Homophobia*

A **phobia** is an irrational fear. **Homophobia** is an irrational fear of homosexuality.

The potential of being gay, or the idea of others being gay, is scary and threatening to some people. Sometimes the fear becomes translated into anger—and even hate. When this happens, homophobia can, and sometimes does, lead to

criminal violence directed against gays and lesbians.

It can also lead to unhealthy attitudes toward one's own sexual orientation.

**HEADS UP!**
If you have homophobic feelings that you think might lead to harming yourself or someone else, it's very important to talk to a counselor (see page 47).

## Gay Parents, Friends, and Family Members

Lots of kids have gay parents, gay older siblings, other gay family members, and gay friends.

PFLAG (Parents, Families and Friends of Lesbians and Gays) is a national organization that provides support for lesbian, gay, and bisexual people and their families and friends. PFLAG's phone numbers are 1-202-638-4200 and 1-202-467-8180. You can call them 9:00 A.M. to 5:30 P.M. (Eastern time), Monday through Friday. (There is a long-distance charge, which will appear on the phone bill.) Or visit their Web site: www.pflag.org.

**HEADS UP!**
Sexual harassment (see page 123) includes inappropriate behavior and remarks regarding someone's sexual orientation. It's possible to express philosophical, cultural, religious or personal viewpoints without harassing (or, for that matter, judging) other people.

# CRUISE CONTROL

It's very appropriate to set limits as to what, if any, physical contact you may have with a partner—now and in the future.

You are responsible for operating within reasonable limits for your age and experience.

Please keep this in mind as you read the material in this section.

## Making Choices

Since people are unique beings, we like different things—different foods, different clothes, different music and movies. People also have different preferences regarding physical touching.

Family values and religious and cultural traditions, as well as health considerations and sexual orientation, play significant roles in the decisions people make about what kind of touching they believe should be included in a sexual relationship with a partner—and when.

All sexual touching requires consent from the people involved (see page 120). Basically, consent is permission freely given by someone who is considered old enough and sober enough to give it (and who is not otherwise impaired). Remember: Each state has its own laws that relate to sexual contact, including sexual contact between consenting juvenile partners. Specific questions? Talk to an attorney who specializes in juvenile law.

## Definitions

Here are expressions you may have heard or may hear other kids talking about.

➤ **Making out** (sometimes called "getting together with") is when two people hug and kiss in a prolonged, romantic way. Sometimes they "French-kiss." French-kissing is open-mouthed kissing, including using your tongue.

➤ **Going further** refers to other ways that people can touch each other sexually while making out. Going further can include caressing any part of the body, with or without clothing. It can include touching the breasts, clitoris, vagina, or behind of a partner; it can include touching the penis and testicles of a partner. It can involve mutual masturbation (masturbating each other).

Making out and/or going further can

## HAZARD LIGHT

Germs can be spread through sexual contact, particularly if someone touches their partner's (or their own) anus and then touches their partner's vagina.

Sexually transmitted diseases (STDs) can also be passed from one person to another during sexual contact. There are many different sexually transmitted diseases (see page 84), and they have a wide spectrum of effects—ranging from physical discomfort to sterility (being unable to make a baby) to permanent physical damage, disability, and even death.

Some STDs are completely curable; others aren't. All are at least treatable, with the goal of managing the symptoms (noticeable signs). None should be ignored.

The sexual contacts defined in this section of *The Guy Book* can potentially put people at risk for becoming exposed to some kind of sexually transmitted disease—if one of the partners happens to be infected (see page 86).

Anal sex, which may cause physical trauma to the anus and surrounding tissue, can put people at an especially high risk for becoming exposed to sexually transmitted diseases, including HIV—the virus that causes AIDS (see page 91).

Oral sex and sexual intercourse are also very high-risk activities for becoming exposed to STDs, including HIV.

The most effective way of avoiding getting a sexually transmitted disease is to not have sexual contact. However, the risk of becoming infected can be substantially reduced by

1) Having sex with only one person, who is having sex only with you.
2) Using a latex condom and water-based lubricant each time you have sex (see page 94).
3) Using an effective barrier during oral sex (see page 91).

Many sexually transmitted diseases are completely curable if discovered early. Some of these have no symptoms. That is why it's critical for people who are having sex to be routinely screened for STDs by a health care professional.

arouse strong sexual responses. Often one or both people have orgasms while making out.

➤ **Oral sex** refers to sexual activity that includes stimulating one's partner's genitals by using the lips, mouth, and tongue.

➤ **Anal sex** refers to partners having sexual intercourse by way of the anus. (This is also referred to as **sodomy**.)

The anus is a very delicate, fragile organ of the body. It's easy to bruise or tear the tissue in and around it. Tears in the tissue can take a long time to heal. They can also provide an entryway for germs and infections. Anal sex presents an **extremely high risk** for getting sexually transmitted diseases.

➤ *Sexual Intercourse*

Vaginal sexual intercourse is a major landmark in a romantic relationship between heterosexual partners (see page 72).

# CHAPTER 10

# *Hazardous Conditions:*
# STDs

Sexually transmitted diseases include genital warts, chlamydia, genital herpes, gonorrhea, syphilis, hepatitis B, AIDS, and others. They're caused by germs—either bacteria or viruses.

Before you read on, keep in mind that most germs that cause STDs die shortly after they leave the comfort of a human being's body. So it would be highly unlikely to catch an STD from, say, a toilet seat.

And you **can't** get an STD from "solo sex" (masturbating by yourself).

### HEADS UP!
Remember: Every attempt has been made to ensure that the info in this book is scientifically correct, but its purpose is to give general information; it shouldn't be relied on as a source of medical advice. If you have symptoms or specific questions, call your doctor or the national STD hot line (see page 90).

► If you haven't yet had sex with a partner, your chances of now having a sexually transmitted disease are approximately zilch.

### *Be informed.*
Vaginal fluid, cervical secretions, menstrual blood, semen, and pre-ejaculate often contain the germs that cause sexually transmitted diseases. Remember: For the germs to be present, the person must be infected.

In some cases, STD germs may be present in sores, warts, bumps, or blisters, or (uncommonly) just plain on the skin. Germs also thrive in mucous membranes, which are the slippery, moist places of the body.

Occasionally, STD germs are present in the mouth, on the lips, or in the back of the throat of an infected person.

### *Bug Deflectors*
When used correctly, latex condoms can provide protection against the spread of many STDs (see page 86). But not all. There are lots of people who have used condoms responsibly but have still ended up getting exposed to an STD—like herpes or genital warts, for example.

## Treating Sexually Transmitted Diseases

Some sexually transmitted diseases, such as syphilis, gonorrhea, and chlamydia, are completely curable provided they are treated in time. Remember: People can be *tested* for STDs, even if there are no outward signs of infection (symptoms).

This is one reason why sexually active people need to **schedule routine checkups**.

## STD OVERVIEW

**Syphilis** is a relatively rare disease. If treated in time, it can be cured. Left untreated, it may eventually lead to death. Symptoms may include a painless, clearly visible ulcer that appears between the legs or on the penis, vagina, anal area (butt), or mouth two to four weeks after sex. This may be followed by feeling sick, getting bumps and spots on the hands and feet, having a rash, and developing a sore throat, sores in the mouth, and lesions between the legs.

**Gonorrhea** and **chlamydia** often have no symptoms or may have very mild symptoms, which can go unnoticed.

**Gonorrhea** may present itself as a yellowy-white, odorless discharge from the penis, pain or burning while peeing, the need to pee often, and/or flulike symptoms. If treated in time, it can be cured. Untreated, gonorrhea can cause a male to become sterile (unable to have children).

**Chlamydia** is especially troublesome, since it is very common and so often has no symptoms. Most young men who contract it don't realize they are infected. They pass it to future partners. Unnoticed (and untreated), chlamydia can spread and cause permanent damage to a woman's reproductive organs (resulting in her becoming unable to conceive a baby). Symptoms for males who do actually have symptoms include having a drip from the penis and pain when pee-

ing. If treated in time, chlamydia can be cured.

Other sexually transmitted diseases, such as **genital herpes** and **genital warts**, cannot be cured, but they are manageable. Early detection helps.

Symptoms of **genital warts**: raised or flat, single or multiple, growths or bumps in the area of the penis, scrotum, or groin (or vulva or vagina in women).

Symptoms of **genital herpes** may include pain and itching—then small, very tender red bumps that become blisters that may appear on the penis, scrotum, buttocks, anus, thighs, or urethra. In women? They may appear on the vaginal area,

vulva, buttocks, anus, thighs, or cervix. These blisters fill with a clear liquid, break, and cause ulcers, then scabs. Ouch!

These breakouts clear up—but may return periodically.

**Chancroid** is a sexually transmitted disease caused by bacteria. It can have symptoms similar to those of genital herpes. The good news is that, unlike herpes, chancroid is totally curable by antibiotics.

## *More? Are you kidding?*

There's a list of other sexually transmitted diseases that don't usually lead to serious medical problems for boys, but they can if left untreated.

Nonspecific urethritis (NSU) is one of these. It causes urinary symptoms, including discharge from the penis, burning when urinating, burning/itching around the opening of the penis, and inflammation of the urethra. Untreated, it can lead to bladder, kidney, and/or urinary tract infections and permanent damage to the reproductive organs.

### HEADS UP!
All painful or troublesome symptoms should be reported to your doctor (see page 20). Remember, *The Guy Book* isn't a medical reference book.

## HITCHHIKERS

As you read the info that follows, don't be surprised if you feel the need to scratch a little; it's a well-known phenomenon that reading about crabs and scabies makes people itch.

## *Crabs*

**Crabs** (pubic lice) are tiny beasts that jump or crawl from one person's pubic hair into another's. They take up residence in this warm, moist nest and multiply faster than rabbits. Symptoms: itch-

ing! Also, they're visible. They can be seen prowling around in pubic hair. After hanging out in pubic hair for a while, they get the urge to travel. They'll break camp and migrate to other favored spots: underarm hair, eyebrows, and eyelashes.

These can be zapped with a prescription lotion from the doctor or over-the-counter medication. Talk to a pharmacist.

## *Scabies*

**Scabies** are frightful little mites that burrow into the skin. They're not necessarily related to sexual activity, but a person could pick them up from sleeping with someone in a scabies-infested bed.

If scabies set up shop in the genital area, they, too, will cause major itching. Scabies can be terminated by a lotion prescribed by the doctor.

## THE TURBO-THREAT— HIV AND AIDS

AIDS (acquired immunodeficiency syndrome) is caused by a virus called HIV (human immunodeficiency virus). AIDS has absolutely swept the earth and millions of people have died from it worldwide. We are just beginning to get a handle on it. As yet, there is no cure for AIDS—only medications to help manage it.

HIV lives in the blood (including menstrual blood), vaginal fluid, and cervical secretions of an infected female. It's also present in the preejaculate, semen, and blood of an infected male. It can be present in the milk of a nursing mother who is infected with HIV.

The HIV virus can be passed from one person to another if any of the above-mentioned body fluids from an infected person enter someone else's body.

The virus can enter a male's body through a break in his skin or through the mucous membranes of his mouth, penis tip, or anus (or nose or eyes). It can enter a female's body through a break in the skin or through her mucous membranes—in her mouth, vagina, or anus (or nose or eyes).

The virus can be passed from an infected pregnant woman to her unborn child, and it can be passed through breast-feeding.

Most HIV infections occur when people have sex without effectively using a **latex** (*not* lambskin) condom, or when people share the needles and syringes used to inject illegal drugs, including steroids.

Anyone—young or old, rich or poor, gay, straight, or bisexual—exposed to the HIV virus can become infected. People who are infected are said to be "HIV-positive." You can't tell by looking at someone if he or she has been infected by HIV. There are no outward clues until a person gets sick, which may be years after the virus has entered that person's body. A person infected with HIV may not know it and can infect others without meaning to.

**HEADS UP!**
Only a test can determine whether someone is infected with HIV. The sooner HIV infection is diagnosed, the better.

**HIV attacks the immune system**—which is the body's system for fighting off infections. Over time, as the body loses the ability to recover from sicknesses, the infected person reaches a point at which he or she is said to have AIDS.

## Don't let your guard down!
Medications that prolong life for people with AIDS are now available. So are medications that help keep the HIV virus from causing full-blown AIDS.

Still, we are not in control of this disease! Results are not as promising as we had initially hoped.

AIDS still must be regarded as potentially fatal. And HIV is spreading at a *very* alarming rate. Our main defense against AIDS still remains not becoming infected with HIV to begin with! Knowing how HIV is spread can help us protect ourselves and one another from contracting this devastating illness.

➤ If you don't have sex with a partner and don't share needles or syringes, and if you avoid contact with other people's blood, you won't be at risk for becoming infected with HIV.

## Symptoms
HIV often causes no symptoms at all. However, it can cause flulike symptoms after someone is initially infected. Later, more symptoms may appear. They include swollen lymph glands in the neck, underarm, or groin area; recurrent fever, which may cause "night sweats"; rapid, unexplained weight loss; diarrhea and decreased appetite; and white spots or unusual blemishes in the mouth. Women may also experience yeast or other vaginal infections that are recurrent or hard to treat.

## HIV and Blood
Skin acts like a protective barrier, but skin can't protect us from HIV if the skin is broken. If skin is scraped, cut, or scratched, or if there is a rash, the virus can easily pass through. Remember that HIV can pass into mucous membranes (even if there is no break in the membrane). Mucous membranes are the slippery-type places on our bodies, like the insides of our mouths, for example.

Coming into direct contact with other people's blood, including menstrual fluid, should be avoided.

Sharing needles or equipment used to shoot up (inject) drugs—including steroids—is a way the virus is commonly passed (see page 56).

Avoid other people's bloody noses, cuts, sores, scratches, bloody tampons, pads, and bandages.

Ear-piercing "guns" and body-piercing equipment must be sterile to prevent transmitting the HIV virus. If you have your ears or body pierced in a store or salon, have your parents make sure that the equipment is properly sterilized. It's safest to have piercing done by a health care professional.

Unsterile tattoo equipment can spread HIV, hepatitis, and other blood-borne diseases.

Should you ever decide to get a professional manicure, be aware that there are guidelines for manicurists. Tools should be sterilized or disposable so that only clean instruments come in contact with nails and skin. Concerned? Bring your own tools.

To stay on the safe side, don't share toothbrushes, razors, or jewelry for pierced ears or body piercing. However unlikely, these things could conceivably have some fresh blood on them; if HIV were present in the blood, it might find an entry point on your body.

## Do you know someone with HIV or AIDS?

Many babies have been born in the United States (and continue to be born in the United States) infected with HIV. This is because some (not all) infected pregnant women end up passing the virus on to their unborn children.

Lots of these children are now in their teens.

If you are infected or know someone with HIV or AIDS, remember that you can't pass it or get it through casual contact, like sitting near, talking to, or hugging an infected person. If you want to show affection in this way, do. People with HIV or AIDS are entitled to support, compassion, understanding, and acceptance—just like everybody else.

## Making Out and STDs

Under certain conditions, making out can pose a risk of exposure to sexually transmitted diseases.

Although hepatitis B is usually spread through sexual intercourse, the virus that causes it may be present in saliva. It's considered technically possible for hepatitis B to be spread by kissing, although it's very unlikely. Talk to your doctor about becoming immunized against hepatitis B— if you haven't already been immunized.

The germs that cause gonorrhea may be present in the back of the throat of an infected person.

A syphilis sore may be present on the mouth of an infected person.

## Herpes: What's Up?

Herpes is in a special category. The basic rule is: The place a herpes sore touches your skin or mucous membrane may become the site where you become infected. Uncommonly, infection can happen without a sore present.

A cold sore on the mouth (oral herpes) isn't considered an STD. But oral herpes can be spread through kissing. **The herpes virus present in a cold sore can be passed to the genitals of a partner during oral sex.** Once spread to the genitals, the partner will have genital herpes.

A herpes sore on the genitals (genital herpes) can be spread to a partner's mouth during oral sex, whereupon the partner will have oral herpes.

Genital herpes can be spread during genital-to-genital contact or skin-to-skin contact in the genital area.

## HIV and Kissing

Small amounts of the HIV virus have been found in saliva, but at the time of publication of this book, there have been no documented instances of HIV having been spread by kissing alone. However, it should be pointed out that HIV could be spread through kissing if blood is present in the mouth of an infected person and saliva is exchanged. (HIV present in the blood could be absorbed by the mucous membranes of the mouth.)

### HEADS UP!

If you have cuts, scratches, or other breaks in your skin—including the skin on the hands—avoid physical contact that would allow another's blood, vaginal secretions, semen, or pre-ejaculate to get on to these breaks. Be aware that "sex toys" (vibrators, dildos, and whatever . . .) can have fluids on them that contain STD germs.

# SEXUAL INTERCOURSE AND STDS

Sexual intercourse is high-risk activity for spreading sexually transmitted diseases, since STD germs may be present in pre-ejaculate and semen, vaginal fluids, menstrual blood, and cervical secretions and in sores, warts, and blisters or on the skin on and around the genitals.

## Oral Sex and STDs

Oral sex is risky activity for spreading STDs. Germs that cause STDs may be present in the mouth as well as in the genitals.

Information about sexual contact and sexually transmitted diseases can be confusing—and can change. If you have specific questions about exposure to sexually transmitted diseases through kissing, making out, "going further," or other contact, you can call the **Centers for Disease Control (CDC) National STD Hot Line**, and they will answer your questions or refer you to someone in your area who can. The call is free, confidential, and won't appear on the house phone bill.

**1-800-227-8922** (U.S. only) 24-7
For the hearing-impaired: **1-800-243-7889** (TTY), 10:00 A.M. to 10:00 P.M. (Eastern time), Monday to Friday
In Spanish: **1-800-344-7432** 8:00 A.M. to 2:00 A.M. (Eastern time), 7 days a week

Or check out their Web sites: www.ashastd.org and, for teens, www.iwannaknow.org
Questions? Send an e-mail to hivnet@ashastd.org
Information about tests for sexually transmitted diseases is available through the local health department, at family planning clinics such as Planned Parenthood (1-800-230-7526), or at a doctor's office (or by calling the CDC National STD Hot Line—U.S. only).

## Oral Sex and HIV

Since HIV may be present in pre-ejaculate and semen, vaginal secretions, and menstrual blood, and since HIV can be absorbed through mucous membranes, which line the mouth, oral sex is in the category of risky sexual contact for exposure to HIV.

### HEADS UP!

Household plastic wrap, a latex condom (see page 94) cut in half lengthwise, or a dental dam can provide a protective barrier to separate the mouth from the vaginal area during oral sex performed on a female, although the effectiveness of this method has not yet been proved.

An infected male can pass HIV and other STD germs to his partner if he doesn't wear a latex condom while oral sex is being performed on him. A condom prevents pre-ejaculate and semen from coming into contact with the mucous membranes of his partner's mouth. It also prevents STD germs that may be present in his partner's mouth from contacting his penis.

## Anal Sex and STDs

To recap, anal sex is very, VERY high-risk sexual activity for becoming infected with HIV and other STDs (see page 86).

A condom can easily break during anal sex. A water-based lubricant (see page 94) spread on the outside of a latex condom (after the condom is on the penis) makes breaking less likely. Again: Do not use petroleum jelly or butter, which can weaken the latex and create a higher likelihood of the condom breaking.

The CDC National HIV/AIDS Hot Line may have other information relevant to protecting oneself and others during sexual contact, including anal sex.

➤ If you have questions about HIV, HIV testing, or HIV/AIDS counseling, call the CDC National HIV/AIDS Hot Line and ask. It's free; the call won't appear on the phone bill. The numbers are:

1-800-342-AIDS (1-800-342-2437)
For the hearing-impaired: 1-800-243-7889 (TTY)
In Spanish: 1-800-344-7432

In Canada, you may consult your local health department, listed in the municipality section of the white pages in the phone book, or call the information operator (411) for an HIV/AIDS hot line.

## HIV and Shooting Up Drugs (Including Steroids)

Since blood from one person can be left in a hypodermic needle and syringe, sharing equipment used to shoot up drugs is a common way for HIV (and other diseases) to be passed from one person to another. And once infected, people can go on to infect their sexual partners as well as those people with whom they may be sharing needles and syringes (see page 56).

## Remember:

People who are sexually active may **reduce** the risk of becoming exposed to HIV by way of sexual contact if:

1. The male wears a latex condom that's been lubricated with a water-based lubricant during every single act of sexual intercourse or anal sex.

2. There is a barrier between partners' mouths and genitals during every single act of oral sex (see above).

3. Partners stay informed regarding new developments and information about HIV and new kinds of protective products and strategies.

**Don't forget:** Other methods of birth control—such as birth control pills—**do not protect either partner** from being exposed to HIV.

# CHAPTER 11

# MAPPING
## *the Journey:*
### BIRTH CONTROL

## RISKS AND RESPONSIBILITIES FOR DISEASE PREVENTION AND BIRTH CONTROL

As you read the material that follows, keep in mind that the most effective way of avoiding unplanned pregnancy is to abstain from having sexual intercourse.

The most effective way to avoid becoming infected with a sexually transmitted disease is to abstain from having sexual contact with a partner.

The topics of disease prevention and birth control should be discussed with parents, a trusted older relative or friend, the school nurse, or a doctor or other health care professional in a family-planning clinic before making a decision about having sex.

Before having sexual intercourse, a visit to a family-planning clinic, the health department, a doctor's office, and/or a drugstore is in order.

Or call Planned Parenthood; they're set up to talk to teens.

PLANNED PARENTHOOD
1-800-230-7526 (toll-free)
Or call 411 for the office nearest you.

### *Condoms*

Most kids have at least heard the word **condom**, but not every kid knows what one actually is.

A condom is a covering for the penis, and a guy wears it while having sex. It's made of very thin, delicate material—usually latex, a kind of rubber. That's why another name for a condom is a "rubber."

Unrolled, a condom looks a little bit like a long, thin, clear, unblown balloon with a very wide opening for blowing it up.

Condoms are used for two purposes: (1) to help prevent the spread of sexually transmitted diseases (STDs) and (2) to help prevent unplanned pregnancy.

## 1. Helping Prevent the Spread of Sexually Transmitted Diseases (STDs)

Remember: Germs for certain sexually transmitted diseases (STDs) can be found in the vaginal fluid, cervical secretions, menstrual blood (all blood, actually), semen, and pre-ejaculate of an infected partner. Some germs can be present in sores, warts, bumps, blisters, or mucous membranes, or on the skin.

A condom provides a thin barrier between a male's penis and the body of his partner. When used correctly, latex condoms help protect both partners from the spread of germs that might enter the body through the mucous membrane at the very tip of the penis, the inside of the vagina, or the inside of the mouth—or through cuts, breaks, scratches, or sores, or by other contact with the skin.

> ➤ But it prevents skin-to-skin contact only between the *shaft* of the penis and the other person's body (see page 4).

If a condom is put on as soon as the penis is erect, a male's **pre-ejaculate** (preseminal fluid), which appears at the tip of a guy's penis when sexually aroused, will be prevented from coming in contact with his partner's body. If ejaculation occurs, the semen will be trapped in the condom.

Not all condoms are made of latex. Those made of natural membrane (lambskin) **are not reliable** for disease protection. Germs can pass through condoms made of natural membrane, including the HIV virus (see page 87).

A condom worn to prevent the spread of sexually transmitted diseases **must be made of latex**. If you (or your partner) is allergic to latex, talk to your health care professional about **polyurethane** condoms.

## ➤ Using a Lubricant

A latex condom needs to be lubricated on the outside (made slippery) in order to make sure it won't tear during intercourse (from friction).

The lubricant *must be water-based.*
Remember: Oil-based lubricants (such as Vaseline or butter) can damage (weaken) condoms and make them more likely to break.

Note: The medications for vaginal yeast infections (which girls get) can also cause a condom (or diaphragm) to weaken.

Water-based lubricants usually come in tubes or little plastic containers. They're sold in drugstores (and sometimes in grocery stores and convenience stores) and usually found near the condoms.

The lubricant is put on the outside of the condom after the condom has been rolled onto an erect penis (see page 99). A water-based lubricant should be used in addition to the lubricant that may already be on a packaged latex condom.

Some water-based lubricants also contain spermicide.

## 2. Helping Prevent Unplanned Pregnancy

Since a condom prevents pre-ejaculate and semen, both of which contain sperm, from landing near or inside a girl's vagina, a condom, if used correctly (with a water-based lubricant), will prevent pregnancy.

It's especially effective for birth control if the female uses **spermicide**, which kills sperm in case the condom leaks or breaks (see page 100).

Condoms and spermicides have another name: **contraceptives**.

### Spermicides

**Spermicides** are products that kill sperm on contact. They also can help knock out some (not all) STD germs. Spermicides come in many different forms: foams, gels, and suppositories. They must be used in combination with a condom in order to be effective for birth control.

The combination of a latex condom worn by the male and lubricated on the outside with a water-based lubricant to help prevent it from breaking PLUS an additional spermicidal foam, gel, or suppository used by the female (put into her vagina before intercourse) both helps prevent pregnancy and reduces the risk of becoming infected with a sexually transmitted disease. This combination is not 100 percent effective, but it is very, very effective if the products are used according to directions. These products don't require a prescription.

And, when used correctly, they're probably the most effective combination of birth control products available that are under the guy's supervision and control; that's why guys need to know about them.

A guy knows if his condom's on right and if it's properly lubricated. Also, he can be present when his partner puts in spermicide.

Since these products are commonly available, relatively affordable, and usually sold with no questions asked, they're a good choice for teen couples who have decided to have sex.

But remember: Condoms can break; spermicide isn't a 100 percent effective backup. Sperm are determined to cause pregnancy, and when you

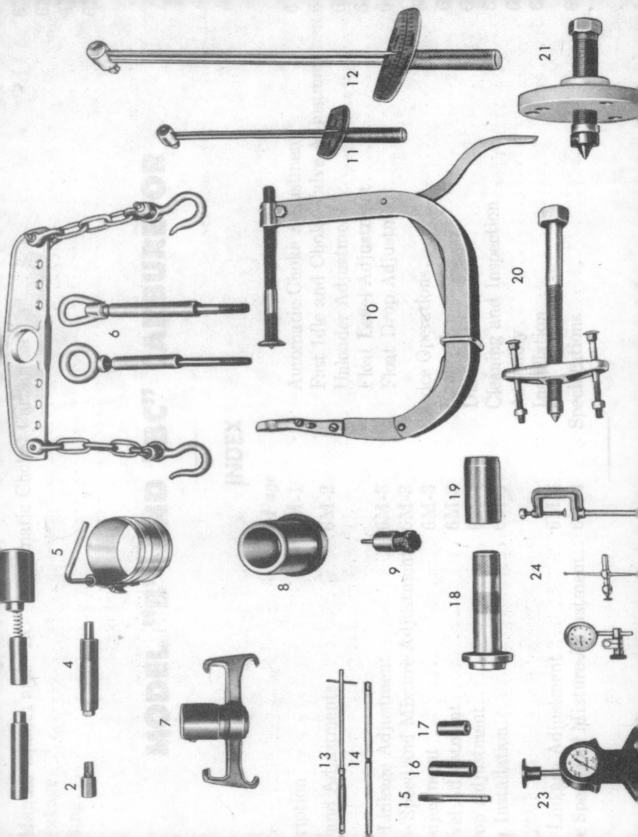

**MODEL 2110 "EC" CARBURETOR**

INDEX

consider that 6 million of them hit the trail at the same time—look out!

Every guy who's having sex with a girl should also know about **emergency hormonal contraception** (see page 99).

There are many other forms of birth control. They are reviewed on pages 101-102. It's your responsibility to discuss birth control with your partner before having sex. It's not "up to her."

And remember even if she's using birth control, condoms are necessary for disease protection! So plan on using them! Age restrictions on buying contraceptives in your state? Probably not. But you can call the drugstore or Planned Parenthood (see page 93) in advance if you want to make sure.

## Condoms: What to Know

A box of condoms often has a romantic picture on the front, such as a man and a woman looking deep into each other's eyes with the moon rising behind them.

The brand name is usually in large print on the box. Inside, condoms come rolled up and individually wrapped in foil or plastic packets. There are also detailed instructions inside the box or printed on an inside wall of the box.

There are many different styles of condoms: lubricated, unlubricated, reservoir-tipped, textured, with spermicide, without spermicide. . . .

As long as the three guidelines below are followed, any style of condoms works (as well as condoms work—which is not 100 percent).

### HEADS UP! Guidelines

**1. The condom should be made of LATEX (not lambskin or natural membrane).**
**2. A "disease prevention claim" should be present on the box. The claim will say something like "These latex condoms, when properly used, may help reduce the risk of catching or spreading many sexually transmitted diseases."**

**3. There should be an expiration date on the box, and it should not have expired.**

➤ **At the time of publication of this book, latex condoms are considered the safest condom choice. However, other materials are being investigated and tested. Stay informed! Talk to your pharmacist or health care professional about any new developments. Or call the STD hot lines on page 90.**

## Shopping for Condoms, Etc.

One fact of life is that if you want to have sex responsibly, sooner or later you're probably going to have to either persuade a friend or family member to score condoms for you—or face up to buying them yourself!

By the time you're old enough to have sex, it probably won't seem like a big deal to walk into a drugstore and buy what you need.

If it does, here's a strategy to keep in mind:

At the time of publication of this book, a box of three condoms costs under $5. Before entering the store, make sure that you have enough money in your pocket or wallet to cover the cost—so you can just bust it out without having to dig for dimes, nickels, and pennies to make the transaction.

➤ **Background Info**
**The cost of condoms depends on how many are in the box. A first-time buyer may want to choose a box of three. (A box of 12 is larger and more expensive, and may draw undue attention to itself or you.)**

**If you should buy condoms from a machine, be aware that condoms shouldn't be stored in hot places or direct sunlight. Where is the machine located?**

## On your mark . . .

The condom section is usually fairly obvious—but of course you'll have to hunt for it.

And naturally, it will hide from you.

In a convenience store, condoms will probably be located near the spot where drugs (like Tylenol) are sold. They may also be found inconveniently near where the cashier is ringing stuff up—a nightmare if the cashier is a cute girl. Or the leader of the church choir.

### . . . Get set . . .

In larger stores—drugstores or grocery stores—condoms will probably be somewhere in the aisles that display drugs, vitamins, Band-Aids, and that kind of thing—not housewares or other stuff.

### . . . Go!

Once you find the condom section, go about your business of picking up the boxes on the display and looking for a box with the magic words "latex" and "disease prevention" on it. Then, find and check the expiration date. It will probably be printed or etched into the side of the box. It will look something like this: JAN 2000-something.

### Bingo

You've snagged some. Maybe they won't ultimately be your favorites, but they'll work. (Save the colored, flavored ones or the ones wrapped in golden, coin-shaped packages for next time.)

You probably won't need to buy condoms marked "large" or "extra large." Unless your penis is HUGE, the regular-size ones should fit. If you get home and discover that regulars can't be rolled all the way down to the base of the penis, you'll have to shop again.

Remember: Condoms are supposed to be tight so they don't slip off!

### One Down, One to Go

On to the area that displays lubricant! Yes—we know that the condom box may say the condoms are already lubricated, but to be safe you still need more, to minimize the chance of the condom breaking from friction during sex.

Water-based lubricant is almost always VERY close to the condoms. Find a product that says "personal lubricant" and "water-soluble" on the box. It will probably say something like "Ideal for use with condoms." (K-Y Jelly, by the way, comes in convenient small tubes, three per package.) The prices will vary, but you should be able to land some for under $5.

Don't get water-based lubricant confused with spermicide; they're two different products.

Nab the lubricant, and you're done.

Unless you need to buy spermicide for your female partner—which will cost about another $5 or so.

In that case, somewhere close to the condoms and lubricants, you will find another section or shelf of products. Look for the word "spermicide" (sperm killer) on a box that also says "vaginal contraceptive foam" (or "jelly" or "suppositories"). It should also say "applicator included" if one is necessary. Check the expiration date. Is it current?

Reel it in.

Mission accomplished.

Now you'll have to bite the bullet and proceed to the cashier. Whatever you do, don't be tempted to stick any of these products in your pocket out of embarrassment and just make a break for the door. Number 1, it's shoplifting, and number 2, contraceptive products usually have little hidden security strips that can set off every alarm in the store.

If you are very, very embarrassed by the prospect of approaching the cashier with these items, try James's old trick, minus the poop medicine (page 68). You can casually shop for this and that—a pack of gum, a magazine, whatever. That

If a condom breaks or leaks, or if another method of birth control (or self-restraint) fails, be aware of emergency hormonal contraception, also known as the emergency contraceptive pill (ECP).

The emergency hormonal contraception pill is not the same as the "abortion pill" (see page 103).

Doctors, hospital emergency departments, and family-planning clinics may be able to provide emergency hormonal contraception for a girl or woman when a couple experiences a condom failure or otherwise has unprotected sex.

If you are aware that your condom has failed, it's your job to tell your partner.

The medication works by either keeping the ovary from releasing an egg or by changing the lining of the uterus so that a fertilized egg cannot attach and develop.

Emergency hormonal contraception is effective only if taken within a certain time frame, and it must be given under appropriate medical supervision. At the time of publication of this book, the time frame is within 72 hours, but check. It may have changed. Regardless, the rule is: the sooner the better! A health care professional must be notified as soon as possible after the unprotected intercourse—even if it happens on the weekend.

Emergency hormonal contraception is not 100 percent effective and is not a routine method of birth control.

Although it can be administered many hours after unprotected sex, its effectiveness diminishes with the passing of time. Questions? Call Planned Parenthood (see page 90 for the number), the emergency room of your local hospital (always open), your doctor's office or family clinic, or the county health department.

way, when you go to buy your contraceptive stuff from the cashier, the condoms won't be lying on the counter all by themselves calling, "Look at me! Look at me!"

They'll be in the company of other objects—innocent ones.

Pay, and you're outta there.

### Test Driving

The first, most useful condom tip is this: A few practice sessions when you are all by yourself are extremely helpful. It's easy to goof up when putting on a condom for the first few times, and it's way better to mess up when there's nothing big at stake.

You will need to have an erection to accomplish this feat.

Don't be surprised if you lose your erection while wrestling with a condom. Until you get the

process down pat, it can throw you off track.

Note that condoms should be stored in a cool place.

### Getting It On

There are instructions enclosed or printed on the inside of almost every box of condoms.

1. Carefully take the condom out of the packet—they're delicate.

A condom should be inspected in good light before putting it on. A condom that's been previously unrolled, is brittle or torn, or is sticky or stuck to itself should be thrown out.

2. Position the rolled-up condom on the top of your penis so that the rolled-up ring is facing out. The rolled-up ring can't be in or you won't be able to roll the condom down. (If your penis is intact, move your foreskin back *first*.)

3. Leave a half inch of space at the tip, hold the

condom by the tip to squeeze out the air, and gently pinch this space closed before and during the unrolling of the condom. This is true even if there is a "reservoir tip." (You also have to pinch closed the reservoir tip.) Why? During ejaculation, there must be some space available inside the condom to hold the semen. Otherwise it will be forced along the sides of the condom and leak out or cause the condom to break.

4. Unroll the condom all the way to the pubic hair, covering your entire penis.

5. If the condom doesn't roll on correctly the first time, begin again—with a new condom. A potentially dinged-up condom is a high-risk item. It belongs in one of two places: in the trash or flushed down the toilet.

## The Real Thing

For a condom to be the most effective for birth control, a guy's female partner should put spermicide in right before sex (see page 95). The spermicide acts as a backup, in case the condom breaks or leaks. Used alone, spermicide is NOT a reliable approach to birth control.

## How a Girl Uses Spermicide

A girl puts in spermicide while lying on her back—just before having sex. She fills the applicator as per instructions that come with the spermicide. She pushes the applicator into her vagina. She pushes the plunger, and the foam or jelly comes out of the applicator. It blankets the walls

of the vagina with a protective shield that kills sperm on contact.

An additional "applicatorful" is required each time intercourse is repeated.

➤ A girl may be interested in helping you put the condom on, but supervise! Most girls don't realize that you have to pinch the tip of a condom to get the air out.

A water-based lubricant must be spread on the outside of the condom, once the condom is completely rolled down over the erect penis. Use it even if the condom is labeled "lubricated" (see page 97). Put the condom on before the penis touches the vagina, mouth, or anus. Don't "poke around" beforehand!

After sex, while the penis is still erect, the male should pull his penis out of his partner's body slowly, holding the condom at the rim with his fingers to avoid spilling semen. He should turn and move completely away from his partner before letting go of the condom.

If there's going to be a victory lap, remember that a new condom, more lubricant, and more spermicide must be used each time a couple has sex.

## Don't just pull out.

A fast way to cause an unplanned pregnancy is to reject using a condom and plan to "just pull out" before ejaculating.

Since pre-ejaculate contains sperm, it's possible to make a girl pregnant simply by having the penis enter the vagina. Also, it's very easy to lose control and—just *not* pull out in time!

If ejaculation happens partway into or even near the entrance to the vagina, look out. Whenever and however semen gets into or near the entrance to the vagina (even on somebody's fingers), there's a potential for pregnancy to happen.

Sperm live for only a few minutes out in the air, but they can live for days (days!) inside of a female's body. **Every time sex happens without using a condom or other form of birth control, there's a significant chance for pregnancy to occur.** Sperm just hang out in there and wait for an egg to show up. Trying to guess when a girl is ovulating and avoiding sex at that time is NOT in itself an effective means of birth control.

Timing intercourse is sometimes called "the rhythm method."

The rhythm method doesn't work reliably, so forget it until you're in a position to raise a child.

### Yup, she can.

Yes, a girl can get pregnant if she is on her period, or if she thinks she is just about to start her period. Yes—a girl can get pregnant if the couple has sex standing up. Yes, a girl can get pregnant the first time she has sex. Yes, a girl can get pregnant if she is using birth control.

> ➤ No form of birth control is 100 percent effective.

### Pregnancy Test Kits

Pregnancy test kits are available in drugstores. They cost about $10. Read the box to find out *when* the test should be taken. To find out results, a girl pees on a little testing device and checks it a few minutes later. Some kits ("early result" kits) can detect pregnancy as early as three days before an expected period. Pregnancy testing can also be done at the doctor's office or at Planned Parenthood (see page 90).

### Positive Result?

If your girl is pregnant, she should not smoke, drink alcohol, or "do" drugs. She needs to make an appointment to see a doctor right away. Meanwhile, she should also call the doctor and ask if it's okay to continue whatever prescription medication or over-the-counter drugs she may be taking *and* find out what she should do to protect the developing fetus from **listeriosis** and **toxoplasmosis**. Among other things, she will be advised not to change the cat litter box, not to play with kittens, not to dig in the dirt without gloves, not to eat raw or undercooked meat or other foods that might contain the bacteria.

## BIRTH CONTROL

A condom is the ONLY form of birth control used for disease prevention. Every other method of birth control requires a condom **in addition** to the birth control to prevent the spread of disease.

### Barrier Methods

Barrier methods physically prevent sperm from coming in contact with an egg. Condoms are worn by the male. There is also a female condom available. The diaphragm and cervical cap are barriers worn by women. Prescribed by a doctor, these small latex cups are inserted into the vagina before intercourse. They fit snugly over the cervix. They are used with spermicide (see page 95).

Diaphragms and cervical caps fail if they don't fit properly, if they are taken out too soon after intercourse, or if the girl doesn't use enough spermicide. The medicine used for yeast infections can weaken a diaphragm (as well as a condom).

### Hormonal Contraceptives

Hormonal contraceptives change the way a female's reproductive system is regulated by hormones, and so prevent pregnancy.

"The Pill" is very, VERY effective—provided the girl takes the Pill every single day at about the same time. Bouts of vomiting and/or diarrhea as well as certain medications (including certain antibiotics) may compromise the effectiveness of the Pill.

Birth control pills are a good deal for a guy. If the girl is using them correctly, that is.

If she's not, he can be having sex with a false sense of security. Even really responsible girls can space out on taking their pills on time and exactly according to directions (if one or more pill is missed). A boy's future may depend on whether or not a girl is using contraception effectively.

Hmmm. Since a guy is morally and financially responsible if he fathers a child, maybe he should stay in charge (see page 103).

**Besides, a condom is necessary for disease prevention.** So why not just plan to use one?

> **➤ See Emergency Hormonal Contraception, page 99. This is different from taking a daily birth control pill.**

## Injectable Contraceptives

Injectable contraceptives are available (they are injected by a health care professional), but they are effective for a shorter time—about three months per injection. Many teen girls choose this method because they don't have to remember to take a pill every day.

Contraceptive implants are injected into the arms of women by health care professionals and last for years.

## Intrauterine Device (IUD)

An intrauterine device is a small device a doctor puts into the uterus of a woman to prevent pregnancy on a long-term basis (until it's removed by a doctor). This is NOT recommended for young women because of the high risk of infection that is associated with its use.

## Surgical Sterilization

Sterilization surgery is permanent. It can be performed on males (**vasectomy**) or females (**tubal ligation**).

A vasectomy is when the vas deferens tubes are cut so sperm can't travel from the testicles to the penis. A tubal ligation is when a woman's fallopian tubes are tied so that a sperm can't reach an egg.

Permanent sterilization surgery is considered inappropriate for young people, who aren't experienced enough to know for sure whether or not they will eventually want to have children. (In some cases, these surgeries are reversible—but successful reversal is not a sure thing.)

## ABORTION

Abortion is not a method of preventing pregnancy. It is a way of actually ending a pregnancy. For some people, there are strong moral, ethical, cultural and/or religious concerns associated with ending a pregnancy once it's begun. Others don't share these concerns.

Most people would agree on this much: If you don't want to have a child, it's far better to avoid becoming pregnant (or causing a girl to become pregnant) in the first place by using birth control or just not having sexual intercourse than it is to have an abortion.

## How do you feel about abortion?

Think about it in advance of having sex with a partner. And find out how your partner feels.

If you're totally against abortion, don't have sexual intercourse unless you're sure your partner shares your viewpoint. Abortion is the girl's (or woman's) choice—not the guy's. A guy can't stop a girl from having an abortion. Neither can he make her have an abortion.

Plus, a girl can change her mind about how she feels about abortion once she finds out she's pregnant.

Currently, girls have two options for abortion:

1. Taking "the abortion pill"—a drug (or, when necessary, a combination of two drugs) that blocks progesterone (a natural hormone needed to sustain a pregnancy) and causes a developing embryo to be expelled from the uterus in the very early stages of pregnancy (within the first seven weeks). This is called having a pharmacological abortion.

2. Having a procedure performed by a doctor. Whether or not the procedure may be performed depends on how far the pregnancy has progressed and the health of the pregnant person.

What basically happens is that the doctor vacuums out, or otherwise removes, the lining of the uterus (which has become the placenta), and the developing embryo attached to it.

Both of the above methods of abortion are relatively safe—but are not risk-free.

> ### ➤ A Review
> **1. Birth control pills:** These pills prevent conception from happening in the first place (used daily).
> **2. Emergency hormonal contraception:** These pills either keep an ovary from releasing an egg or keep a fertilized egg from implanting in the uterine wall (should be used within about 72 hours—the sooner the better).
> **3. Pharmacological abortion:** This method uses pills to cause a pregnancy to fail and the uterus to expel the embryo that has already been implanted (must be used within 49 days of the first day of a girl's last period).

## If She Keeps the Baby

If a girl decides to have the baby, the guy has rights and responsibilities—once the baby is born. Rules vary from state to state.

## Rights Vary from State to State

The dad may be given permission to visit the child throughout the child's childhood and teens.

If the girl (or woman) decides not to raise the child once it's born, the father may be given the chance to demonstrate that he can raise the child himself or with the help of his family.

He also may ask to have a say in whether or not the baby will be placed in a foster home or placed with an adoptive parent or parents.

## Responsibilities Vary from State to State

The father may be held legally responsible for the financial support of his child until his child becomes an adult (reaches age 18).

If the mom and baby are financially helped by a government agency (welfare system), the government may ask for reimbursement from the father.

The mom may sue the father of the child for continuing child support. Adjustment of the payments may be made as the dad's salary increases.

## The Most Awesome Responsibility of All

The dad will have put a kid on the planet. The kid will reasonably have expectations that his dad will be his daddy.

# CHAPTER 12

# DRIVER
## *Etiquette:*
# RULES OF THE ROAD

### Someone to Roll With

Sure, it feels great to be popular, but it isn't necessary to be in the center of a social scene (or even to be included in a popular group) to be happy and fulfilled by friendship.

One or two really good friends to roll with is all you'll ever need.

> ➤ **Remember: To have a good friend, you need to be a good friend.**

### Being There

If you're not sure how to respond to a friend who's feeling down, that's okay—being there is a good start. Hanging out with your friend—just being physically present—may be all that's called for in the situation.

Doing something together (like playing catch or going for a walk) is another way to show you care.

Listening helps; you're not required to have the answer to the problem. If you do want to advise or make a comment, try to imagine yourself receiving that bit of advice in just the same way you intend to give it and see how it feels—before you say it to your friend.

**HEADS UP!**
Worried? Trust your instincts. Your friend's telling you about the situation may be his or her way of asking for help. If your friend's problem is serious, encourage him or her to talk to a trusted adult and/or refer him or her to the hot lines in this book (see page 46). And talk to a trusted adult yourself, even if you promised you wouldn't.

## GUY REPORTS: THREE STRATEGIES FOR GETTING NOTICED

**#1:** "My first scheme wasn't very romantic. It was a scheme to get the birthday girl at a party to notice me. It was totally unpremeditated. I went around and stomped on some of her birthday balloons.

"I got the girl's attention as well as everyone else's.

"I realized afterward that it was a dumb thing to do."

**#2:** "Two young beauties about my age (14) were sitting down by the boat dock, at Jump-Off Joe, where my family was vacationing.

"I had my own fly rod and a new green-and-black woodsman shirt. I put on my shirt, got my rod, and strolled down to the dock, where nobody had caught a fish in a hundred years.

"I started shooting out some long casts and doing some tricky retrieves. I worked out to the end of the dock and after a few more casts, was knee-deep in water.

"As it turned out, I was standing on a boat-launching machine and was being launched.

"I decided that rather than lose my cool and scramble back up on the dock, I would continue my performance. I refused to look back. At sunset, with my head and shoulders above water, I made my last cast."

This may be your best bet:

**#3:** "I just sidled up to 'em and hoped they'd notice me."

### Teasing

Teasing is a timeworn (or is it just worn out?) way of guys getting girls to notice them.

Teasing is hurtful. Don't tease.

If you can't help yourself, you should know that teasing shouldn't ever include remarks about a person's physical appearance. Sexual harassment is pretty big territory, and it does include making jokes and wisecracks that focus on sexual characteristics, even if the comments are meant to be complimentary (see page 123).

### No Visual Inspection

You're probably attracted to a certain body type; most guys are. But appreciating a girl's body is not the same as evaluating, sizing up, or rating her figure. Who likes to be inspected? Nobody.

### Honking Your Horn/ Backfiring

Loudly farting and belching may be a competitive sport, and it may be somewhat impressive, but, well, duh. Don't rely on it to get the attention of somebody you have a crush on.

### Pileups

Boisterous roughhousing with other guys is universally and historically a way that boys try to get girls to notice them. Wrestling, hat snatching, chasing each other, and rolling in the dirt are among the favored maneuvers.

How effective is this behavior in gaining a girl's attention?

Not very. But it's fun!

A swarm of boys gathered by an outside trash can in the school yard karate-kicking yellow jackets isn't a bad thing.

But it's not like a cute girl is going to come up to you when you've just successfully nailed one and say, "E-e-e-yeah!"

If you want to capture the attention of a girl,

you've got to buckle down and actually make the commitment to communicate.

At least say hi.

## Bonjour!

A friend told me that when he was in junior high, he went to the beach. While sitting in the sand, he noticed two cute girls, about his age, sunning themselves on a blanket nearby. They were wearing bikinis and lying on their bellies. He couldn't help but note that they had unclipped the straps of their bathing suit tops to avoid getting tan lines.

My friend sat pensively looking out at the waves. How could he get to talk to them?

He could barely hear what they were saying, but he was able to identify that they were speaking French.

*Fantastique!*

He'd already had a few French lessons!

After a while, my friend got up his nerve and casually wandered over.

*"Bonjour,"* he said in his best French accent.

Both girls popped up and cheerily said, *"Bonjour!"*

They sat there, smiling at him.

Inspired by the experience, he took French every year in school from then on.

# CRUISING

Into girls? The following section covers a few things you might want to keep in mind.

## *Actually Getting to Know Her*

Most parents set age limits on dating, and most preteens and young teens aren't allowed to date. But preteen kids who like each other romantically often talk on the phone and spend time together in groups. For example, at school activities; at a church, temple, or community center; at sports events; or at restaurants, the movies, or the mall.

It might seem hard to talk to a girl at first, but when you're in a group, it's easier because there are other kids to interact with at the same time.

But what do you say?

Just talk. Don't use standard "pickup lines." Girls don't fall for these much. (Nobody does.)

You can start by asking her questions about herself, but not overly personal ones. Find out what she's into—sports, music, whatever. The conversation will build from there.

You might ask for her phone number—if she gives it to you, you can call her up. Don't call before about 9:00 in the morning or after about 9:00 P.M. It may wake up younger siblings or otherwise annoy her parents.

If you call when she's not home, leave your number so she can call you back. If she doesn't, it's probably fine to call back once more and leave your number.

After that, if she doesn't return your call, it probably means that she doesn't want to talk to you on the phone, after all. She may have given you her number, but she changed her mind. So stop calling.

If it turns out that she actually was out of town or away from the house for an extended period of time, she'll end up calling you eventually.

If she doesn't give you her number but asks for yours, that's not a bad sign. Lots of girls don't give out their numbers. Maybe she'll call you, and maybe she won't. If she does end up calling you, you'll know it's because she *wants* to talk to you—rather than just having happened to pick up the

## GUY REPORTS: FIRST DANCE

I interviewed a 21-year-old about his first school dance.

"My first school dance? Yeah, I remember it. It was in the sixth grade."

I said, "I want you to think about it and try to remember details. I need information for my book for boys."

My friend then told me he didn't have to think to remember. He remembered the whole thing perfectly, from beginning to end: "Me and three of my friends stayed by the wall for the whole dance."

"That was it?"

"Yup. We just stood there the whole time, at the wall. It was fun."

"It was?"

"Yeah."

"Did you interact at all with the girls?"

"Yeah. We tossed pieces of broken cookies at them. They liked it."

"They did?"

"I think so."

"Well, when did you actually get up your nerve and ask one of them to dance?"

"About five years later."

phone and discovered that you're on the other end of the line.

During a conversation, on the phone or in person, it's fine to talk about yourself, but also steer the conversation in her direction.

Be *very* careful not to talk negatively about her family, her friends, your friends, or kids you both know—this will come back to bite you.

## If the opportunity arises, you can always ask:

Is she going to the dance?

Slow dancing may be the first romantic physical contact a boy makes with a girl. When you are slow dancing with someone, your heads may be close together. Your cheeks may be touching. Your heart may flutter. Or pound is more like it.

Holding someone in your arms and dancing can be a way of expressing sexual feelings; it may be the first romantic encounter you have with a partner.

Wait a minute!

If you're 13 and haven't completed (or even started) your growth spurt—and you're slow dancing with a girl—it just may not be cheek to cheek. It might be cheek to chest. (Uh—that would be your cheek on her chest.)

This minor detail shouldn't keep either one of you from having a good time dancing with each other.

Who says a guy has to be taller than a girl, anyway?

## Slow-Dancing Instructions

If you're at a dance or party and don't want to wait 5 years to dance with a girl but don't actually know how to dance, here are some tips for first-timers:

1. Walk up to a girl and say, "Want to dance?" When starting out, it's not a bad idea to ask a girl who's a friend—rather than someone you have a crush on. That way, you can practice with somebody you feel somewhat comfortable with.

2. If she says yes, then take her by the hand. You may want to lead her deep into the group of people who are dancing. That way, you'll feel less conspicuous.

3. If you turn to her and hug her—gently, with your arms around her waist—she'll undoubtedly hug you gently back, with her arms around your neck. Your face will be close to her face, or touching it.

Or you can hold her right hand with your left hand and dance with your right hand on her back, and she'll dance with her left hand on your back.

4. Keep on gently hugging her as you slowly move to the music. If you haven't danced slow with a girl before, it works just fine to just sort of rock back and forth. Most of us have some natural instincts about dancing if we just relax and listen to the music. Don't look at your feet.

Don't dance to the saxophone! Dance to the drums or whatever instruments seem to actually have some kind of a predictable rhythm going on.

If you feel brave, walk around a little bit while hugging. The girl will follow along. (Or try to.)

The tradition is, the boy "leads" and the girl follows his lead. But there isn't a law against the girl leading and the boy following.

## But what if she says no?

If the girl says no, politely accept her rejection. Return to where you were standing. Your friends can have opportunity to cheer you up by making fun of you and punching you on the shoulder.

## ASKING FOR A DATE

When you ask for a date, you should look for some kind of a green-light response. If somebody says, "Sorry. I'm busy," and leaves it at that, that's a no.

## CHEAT SHEET: DATING TIPS
### Essential pointers:

• Checking out other people when you're on a date won't exactly boost your date's confidence.

• Have an opinion on how fast or how much your date is eating? Save it.

• If you're into someone, go for the gold. Don't try to get in through the grapevine by dating a friend or relative first. It will put you "off limits" for the future.

• Kissed your date? Even though it's tempting to talk it up with your buddies, don't. Talking about it sends a message: Your date isn't worth keeping your mouth shut for.

• Have a cell phone? Switch it to OFF and pay attention to your date.

• Find out you're wrong in an argument? Credit goes to the winner.

• Be considerate—but not selfless! You count, too. Don't be a doormat or servant for your date.

• Wondering what your date would like to do? Ask. But have some of your own ideas on where to go and what to do.

• No need to be the strong, silent type all the time. Communicating your feelings will encourage your date to communicate with you.

• Being overly possessive and jealous will work against you.

• There's a time and place to verbalize your obsession with celebrity beauties. It's not good to do this on a date.

• Watch your slang. Certain expressions for body parts are offensive.

• Shallow? Making negative comments about people's bodies tends to project the image that you have a superficial view of people.

• Narrow? Racist/religious/cultural/gay "jokes" and slurs reflect ignorance and hurt everybody. Your date won't be impressed.

• Nervous? Don't forget to smile.

• When you really care, it shows. Ask how your date is doing and then listen to the answer.

• Be yourself. How else will your date know the real you?

• An occasional gift is a good thing; don't overdo it.

However, if someone responds with: "Sorry. I'm already busy. What about next weekend?" that's a green light. Try again.

If someone says, "Ohmygosh! I'd so love to but, uh . . . I have to, like, wash my dog," take it as a no. If the person even owns a dog, this urgent dog bath could easily be postponed. Besides, you wouldn't want to be placed in line behind a stinky dog—if it were actually true.

If someone has an actual reasonable reason to say no, it's fine to ask for a date on a different night.

## Oh, yeah!

Okay. So you get a yes.

Now what? Be sure to discuss the plan, especially the transportation part, in advance—so your date will be able to clear it with a parent. And know when to be ready.

If you're arriving at the house or apartment, rather than meeting someplace, go up to the door. Don't honk, whistle, or call on a cell phone from the driveway.

If the parent is home, say hi and tell the parent where you're going and what time you expect to return.

If you're the inviter, plan to pay.

It's an unfair and annoying convention (to both genders) that the guy should somehow be the one to pay—or even the one to do the inviting. But this convention persists. Remember that being traditional is a choice, not a requirement.

If your date *offers* to pay or pay half, that's okay, too. Also, if your date has invited you out, your date should be planning to pay! (Or at least planning to pay half.) Some couples take turns paying when they go out.

Unless you're eating at a fast-food restaurant, leave a tip. It's unclassy to stiff a server. Leaving 20 percent of the total bill is a good tip in most places.

Most dates like to get something to eat, talk, walk around, and hold hands in a setting where there are other people around. A movie or a school, community, or sports event is a good place to go on a first date.

Bowling alleys, skating rinks, miniature golf courses, and family fun centers are places young teens seem to like. But be on the lookout for sleazeball adults who frequent these places *because* young teens seem to like them so much!

Get your date back on time so parents won't worry and/or get mad.

## Kiss good-bye?

The actual truth is this: Just about every girl who walks the earth knows how to signal to a boy that she'd like to be kissed. Then again, she just might go for it and kiss the boy herself.

Almost every girl also knows how to signal that she doesn't want to be kissed.

You've got radar; we all do. Just read the signals.

And you know what? You can always just straight-up ask her. Lots of guys do.

## Decoding

If you and your date have had a good time and you're unclear as to whether or not you might kiss each other good-bye, and don't want to ask, here are a few things to consider:

When it's time to say good-bye, if she searches your eyes for a minute or watches your mouth while you're saying you had a good time, it's probably okay to try for a kiss.

If you bump noses, that's fine because it happens all the time.

If she looks down, turns her head away from you, hurries to find her key, or makes a grab for the doorknob, better luck next time. Say good night.

Wait till she gets into the house and shuts the door before you leave.

# THE INNER CIRCLE

Maybe you've found a girl that you like spending time with, and she invites you to her house. Here're a few pointers to help prepare for the test.

## *Meeting Her Family*

When you are relatively young and want to spend time with a girl you like, without being in a group setting, it's probably going to involve seeing her at her house. An event that is sometimes dreaded by guys is meeting the family of a girl they like—especially her parents.

House rules and customs vary in our multicultural society. But here are ten good rules to guide you. If you follow them, you're bound to make an excellent impression:

1. Unless you wear it for cultural or religious reasons, take off your cap/hat/beanie when you enter the house. If you are invited to leave it on, then put it back on if you want to.

2. If you are sitting down when introduced to a family member, stand up. After saying hey, hi, or hello and/or shaking hands, it's fine to sit back down again.

3. You don't have to talk your head off, but try to answer questions asked, as long as they're not too personal. "Please" and "thanks" are essential for showing that you have good manners, and you get lots of points for using these words.

4. Ask permission if you want to use the phone. (Unless, of course, it's an emergency of some sort.) Avoid making long-distance calls, if possible.

5. Don't assume it's okay to visit with your girl in her bedroom, because it's probably not going to be. In some cultures this is absolutely, positively not okay. If it is allowed, make sure that the door remains open.

Generally speaking, parents don't like guys in a room with their daughter when the door is closed—especially not the bedroom. They may not say this, but they expect you to know this and will undoubtedly hold it against you if you do it.

6. If you are in your girl's room visiting, you can chill on the floor, chair, couch, beanbag, box, or bench—but don't stretch out on the bed like you belong there. Parents usually don't like this.

7. Clean up. Throw out empty wrappers; bring empty cans, bottles, or glasses you've used into the kitchen.

8. Don't criticize your girl's family members or make fun of the family pets. If she does, just listen. Don't agree.

9. Avoid outward displays of affection, especially if you are in the girl's home for the first time. Kissing your girl hello or good-bye in front of her parent isn't a good idea, especially in the beginning.

10. When you leave, locate the parents (unless they've gone to bed) and say good-bye and thanks.

## *Sit-Down Dinner Regs*

If you are invited to eat with the family at the table in a formal family setting, etiquette will vary according to culture. Keep your eyes open and watch what others are doing.

Generally speaking, here are ways to make a good impression:

• Unless your hat is on for a cultural or religious reason, make sure you're not wearing it at the table.

• If there's a napkin at your place, put it on your lap after you sit down.

• It is extremely polite and helpful to help seat an elder; if a very old (or disabled) person is going to be sitting next to you and needs assistance, help with the chair. Pull it back from the table, wait for the person to sit down, and help scoot it in (gently).

• If food is served by *passing serving plates* and bowls around the table:

When you are passed a serving plate or bowl, offer to hold it for whoever is sitting next to you, especially if it's an elder. Wait for him or her to serve him- or herself before you put food on your own plate. And, if there's a really little kid next to you, help him or her with the serving. If food is served by someone at the head of the table onto plates that are then passed, keep passing the plates past you until you end up with one.

• If a prayer is said before eating, listen. It's not necessary to do anything whatsoever during grace except remain quiet (don't eat).

• Generally speaking, it's best to wait until an adult at the table starts eating before you start eating. But do look around to see if others have started. In some cultures, it's considered an insult to let the food get cold.

• There is a lot of variance in cultural standards of politeness regarding the mechanics of eating. Regardless, take medium-size bites. Don't stab huge chunks of food with your fork and bite from them. Cut into bite-size pieces first. Try not to herd food onto your utensils with your finger. And hey! You! Look up occasionally when you eat; it's not polite to stare continuously at your plate.

Picking up certain food with your fingers to eat it is okay in most situations. Ribs, moo shu pork rolled in a pancake, fried chicken, flautas, tacos, and other mmm-mmm delicious foods are traditionally eaten with the fingers. Don't do it if you're invited to eat with the queen of England,

though. With Her Majesty present, every last thing has to be eaten with a knife and fork—except maybe your roll!

Avoid talking with your mouth full—although we do know that people inevitably ask questions of other people who have just loaded the food in.

• Okay (in fact, good—the chef will like it) to have seconds if offered, but stay tuned in to how much food is available for how many people. If there's not much, just take a little bit more. Tip: Don't talk about calories, fat grams, or dieting while people are eating. It spoils the fun.

• If someone starts clearing plates into the kitchen, at least make a gesture toward helping. The point is: You're not really there to be "served" by your girl's parents. Unless somebody tells you not to, carefully clear the plates (without stacking them).

• Under no circumstances should you leave your plate, utensils, and dirty napkin sitting on the table if you are completely done eating and getting up from the table; remember, you're not at a restaurant.

• Thank the provider for the meal.

• When you leave the table, push your chair in.

• Offer to help with the dishes.

## Very Formal

Dah-ling! If there are two forks, use the one with the shorter prongs for salad and dessert. The long prongs are for the main dish.

If there are two spoons, the big one is for soup or broth or dessert (ice cream, say) and the small one is for putting sugar into coffee or tea at the end of the meal—or helping yourself to small blobs of mustard, jelly, etc.

If there are small bread plates at the table, yours is the one to your left—nearest your fork.

Break pieces of your roll or French bread before eating and butter/jelly up each piece separately; don't sink your teeth into the whole roll at once. And don't slather the whole piece of bread with butter or jam.

Pass the salt and pepper together if someone asks for one or the other, and don't nab salt, pepper, soy sauce, or other spices. If someone at the table has asked for something to be passed, you're not supposed to hijack it!

When you're done eating your main course, neatly place your long-pronged fork and knife right next to each other, touching, pointing to the middle of the plate.

Keep your short-pronged fork for dessert.

> ➤ If there are chopsticks instead of forks, knives, and spoons, use those for everything except for broth (you will be given a spoon for this). Remember not to serve yourself with the ends of the chopsticks that you eat from. Serve yourself with the large serving utensil provided, or, if there isn't one, flip your chopsticks around and serve yourself with the squared-off ends that haven't touched your mouth.

## IT'S A FORMAL AFFAIR

It's unlikely that you'll be attending an actual formal before, say, midway through high school or later (or it could be never—some people are able to escape these things altogether!), but for future reference:

It can take *days* to prepare. You'll probably want to enlist your parent to help you.

You'll need to know who your date is going to be well in advance of the occasion. So . . . ask!

### Penguin Suit

If "black tie" (tux) is called for, you'll probably have to go to a rental shop a total of three times: once to order and get a fitting, once to pick up the tux, and once to return it.

Start by calling a rental shop and asking how much lead time they'll need to fit you, and ask about how much you can expect to pay for a (standard) rental. Call around to do some comparison shopping. There should be at least *something* available in the $50-to-$70 range, which should include a white dress shirt, "studs" and cuff links, bow tie (already tied), jacket, pants, and a choice of either a plain vest or a cummerbund (fabric

belt). Patent-leather shoes may cost an additional fee. You can save some money by wearing plain black leather dress shoes if you own them or can borrow them. Just make sure they're polished and in good shape.

When you choose a tux, unless you have a particular "look" in mind, it's safest to tell the salesperson you want to stick with traditional black-tie attire. Your look will be understated—and you'll for sure be classy, stylin', and cool. (The general idea is for the guy to not upstage his date.)

It may be worth buying the insurance (about $7 to $10 additional in most places), if you even *think* you and your friends might get into a spontaneous wrestling match just before or during the event. If you rent a white tux, by all means get the insurance.

If you are more the artist type and want to make a more alternative clothing statement, you may want to rent a tux from a vintage-clothing store. Call around and see what's available.

### Corsage/Boutonniere

A corsage (a little pin-on bouquet of flowers and ribbon) or wristlet, described below, will be expected by your date if your date is a girl.

Guys wear boutonnieres. A boutonniere is usually a single flower specially prepped for (one hopes) easy pinning to your left lapel. Your date will be responsible for getting you one.

The corsage/boutonniere exchange happens upon your arrival at wherever you're meeting or picking up your date. The flowers should be kept in a cool place, but not necessarily the refrigerator. Ask the flower salesperson about this.

It's your date's job to pin on your boutonniere. This is an act of faith. With luck, you won't get stabbed. The pin goes through the little wrapped boutonniere stem, through the fabric of the lapel, and then out through the wrapped stem again.

A "wristlet" is a corsage attached to an elastic bracelet, and it's worn on the girl's (left) wrist. A wristlet is a mighty good idea, since it isn't pinned on and you won't have to worry about wrinkling, snagging, or rumpling your date's dress. If a corsage is the flower arrangement of choice, it's pinned above the girl's left breast. Good luck—because you, too, may become the designated pinner (if her mom or big sis isn't available to do the job).

A wristlet, like a corsage, generally costs between $10 and $15.

## Ordering the Flowers

Ask your date what color dress she's planning to wear, because the flowers should generally match it. Make sure you order a corsage or wristlet that won't clash with her dress. (Example: If her dress is red, don't order a corsage of pink and orange flowers. You can discuss all this with the salesperson.)

Visit a flower shop (or grocery store that makes flower arrangements) about a week in advance. With help from the salesperson, you can decide on the flowers and establish the pickup time, which will usually be on the morning of the event.

## Photo Ops

There is often a photographer at a formal dance, ready to take your picture under some kind of a gazebo or another—and collect about $25 from you and/or your date. Photos are optional.

Also, either or both sets of parents will probably be waiting in the wings at home to snap a few pics before you roll. Say *cheese*! Formals are very time-consuming and expensive, and all the parents have to show for their effort and dough are a few lousy snapshots!

So cooperate!

## Hmmmm

Let's see:
    Tux: $65
    Tickets: $50
    Flowers: $15
    Photos at the event: $25
    Something to eat before or after the event: $40
    Do you *really* want to rent a limo?

## The Ride

Limos are justifiably discouraged (even banned) by many schools because of the expense and one-upping involved.

However, if you're planning to share a limo with another couple or couples, also call around and ask the per-hour rate. Discuss payment arrangements with the company—in advance.

Make sure that one responsible person collects the money from everybody before the event. Otherwise, someone is bound to get stiffed for the money—and it's probably whoever made the arrangements originally. Don't forget the tip (about 15 percent) for the driver.

The driver will open the door for everybody, including the guys. Keep in mind that being classy involves being polite and considerate to people who are "serving" you—in this case, the driver.

## Arrival and Departure

When you arrive, compliment your date. Your date will probably be a little nervous about getting all dressed up—just like you are. Hearing a compliment is very reassuring. Especially after all the shopping and getting ready!

Of course, walk your date to the door when it's time to go home.

Whether or not you kiss good-bye is up to both of you. It will either happen or not.

## Prom Versus Morp

Do you know that some schools have an alternate event called a morp on prom night? This event is for kids, boys and girls, who like to socialize but hate proms, hate getting dressed up, can't afford formal events, can afford a formal event but have more important things to spend the money on, or don't have a date for the prom.

Kids arrive casually dressed (in pajamas at some schools) and sit around till the wee hours of the morning in the gym or cafeteria and eat pizza and other food provided by parent sponsors, listen to music, watch videos, talk, hang out, and complain about proms.

Sound like fun?

Talk to your student council rep about organizing one.

## MOVING ON

Initiating a breakup with someone is never easy, but it's possible to be classy about it. Keep in mind the ol' golden rule: Treat others with the same degree of respect and consideration you'd like to be given yourself—under similar circumstances.

Breakups can be hard for both parties. Remember to communicate with your parents and/or other trusted adults during stressful times. Most adults have been on both sides of a breakup at some point or another, and can be really helpful and understanding.

## Taking Another Route

If you are in a relationship, particularly a sexual relationship, and your romantic interests have shifted to someone else, it's advisable to break up before actually pursuing another love interest. Rejection is an emotion we all need to cope with in some way or another as life goes on. But feeling both rejected and cheated on can make rejection harder to accept and may also make it harder to trust someone else in the future.

## What do you say?

## Someone else in the picture?

"I don't want to be in a relationship" is fine—if it's true. But if you're planning to immediately start dating someone else, it's probably better to come clean. "I'm interested in seeing someone else," or "I'm attracted to someone else" may be hard to hear, but if it's true—you've been truthful. And you've given your ex a heads up for the future.

## Just want to "uncouple"?

Most people would agree that it's best to be honest about your feelings. You shouldn't be given a citation for not telling the whole and complete truth, and a lengthy explanation shouldn't be required. But it's hurtful to be straight-up lied to. Examples: "I've suddenly decided to become a priest." (Really? But you're not even Catholic!) "I can't go out with you anymore because you're just too good for me." (Yawn. Nobody—and I mean *nobody*—falls for this one.)

Before speaking, take a minute to think how you would feel receiving the information yourself.

Would you rather hear "My feelings have changed" or "You're not attractive anymore"? Probably neither one—but given the choice?

Talking about your own feelings can be the best way to go (I feel this way or that way. . .). Talking about or criticizing the other person (you do this, you do that . . .) may not be as effective.

Example: "I feel trapped in this relationship" is an alternate way of saying "You're too possessive! You act like you own me!"

## Just Friends?

"I just want to be friends" is fine—if it's true. Many couples remain in good standing with each other and go on to being just friends.

But not every former couple can manage this type of change, at least not at first. Don't be surprised if your ex says no to being "just friends." And if you don't think you want to continue a relationship as friends, avoid proposing it. "I think it would be best if we don't see each other for a while" is fine.

## When and where?

Many people consider it classier to break up in person than on the phone or in a letter or e-mail (unless you've moved or live far away).

Having a friend break up for you can be pretty tacky. So is breaking up right in front of other people. Avoid it if possible.

## How's your timing?

Can some recovery time possibly be built into the plan? For example, a Saturday afternoon at your soon-to-be ex's house (where support is available) may be better than springing a breakup on a Monday morning at school. Breaking up just before a really important event, performance, or exam may be regarded as sabotage.

# CHAPTER 13

# THE
# *Right of Way:*
# CONSENT

## *An Age Issue*

Sexual contact between two kids who aren't in a similar age group may be regarded as a form of child abuse, even when both kids agree to it.

## *Why?*

When one kid is significantly older than another, the older one is felt to have an advantage over the younger one, especially at certain critical stages of physical and emotional development. So even if the younger person agrees to sexual contact, we don't consider him or her to have had a fair choice.

In other words, the two aren't equals—they don't have equal experience in the world. If the younger one says yes, we presume that the older one has influenced the decision. So we don't count it as consent.

## *What does "similar age group" mean?*

Rules vary from state to state.

Romantically involved with someone older or younger?

Questions or concerns?

Call the Child Help USA Hot Line to discuss your situation (see page 134 for information about this 24-hour hot line, which is staffed by professional counselors).

## *More About Consent*

Our laws protect all people of all ages from being forced (by either physical force or verbal threat) into sexual contact. This is true even if they have agreed to have sexual contact with each other in the past.

A person who is very drunk or stoned is not in any condition to give consent. Consent given by a drunk or stoned person doesn't count (see page 125).

Consent is valid provided the person is in a similar age group and is not impaired by alcohol, drugs, or disability—or has not been in any way coerced (tricked, blackmailed, threatened, or unfairly manipulated in some other way) into giving consent.

## "No" Never Means "Yes"

Once given, consent may be withheld or withdrawn by either partner at any time. As soon as one person says no, the other person *has* to stop. That's the rule, and that's the law.

➤ **In the Movie**

We've all seen this one:

In the movie, the beautiful, sexy woman fiercely resists being kissed and then gives in—passionately!—once a handsome, buff male forces the issue (by maybe grabbing her shoulders and pulling her close to him and kissing her anyway). She's "swept away" by the heat of the moment and melts in his arms. She really, truly does want him—in the movie.

In real life, she really, truly doesn't want him.

In movies, actors may be considered sexy when they force themselves on women. In real life, this has a different name: sexual assault.

Overpowering anyone—male or female—who doesn't want to be kissed or otherwise touched in a sexual way is against the law.

## Back off.

When one person says or otherwise indicates no, it means one thing: No. This is true for all couples: preteens, teens, and adults. It's even true for married couples. Becoming physically aggressive with a person who doesn't want to have sexual contact or who wants to end sexual contact is totally against the law.

And there are lots of ways people indicate no without saying the word "no."

Examples? "I don't want to do this"; "I'm not ready for this"; "My mom wouldn't want me to do this"; "I don't feel right about this"; "Stop"; "I think we should stop"; "I'm scared"; "Don't"; "That hurts." These all mean: No.

## Signaling No

There is also body language that indicates no.

Examples? Pulling away, pushing away, turning the head away (to avoid being kissed), struggling to get free of someone's grip.

## Mixed Messages

A mixed message should also be interpreted as no.

What is a mixed message? It's when someone signals both yes and no, or if the other person interprets the signals to be both yes and no.

### HEADS UP!
### Yes + no = no.
An example:

A girl sits down very close to a boy on a couch. He puts his arm around her shoulder. She tips her head onto his chest and then looks up at him, directly into his eyes. He leans closer to kiss her—but she turns her head away from him.

She smiles a little, snuggles up closer, and looks up at him again.

Has she changed her mind?

Who knows!

Is it okay for him to try one more time to kiss her?

No, it's not.

Unfair?

Some people would think so.

Regardless, it's a no.

By turning her head away, the girl has indicated that she doesn't want to be kissed. Apparently, she just wants to sit by him and look into his eyes.

Is she just being playful?

How do you know?

You don't, and you can't. So take it as a no.

Any form of a no means no, and stays no regardless of when and how it's given. A mixed message also means no—and stays no.

After a no or a mixed message, it's up to the person who says no to make the next move, if there's going to be one.

Have a girlfriend who's giving you mixed messages? Confused?

Talk to her about it. Words are more reliable than signals. Straight-up ask her: What's going on? Is this okay—or isn't it?

# WRONG WAY: SEXUAL HARASSMENT

The material that follows deals with sexual harassment, which consists of comments and behaviors that are harmful to the development of a positive, healthy attitude toward one's own body, sexuality, or sexual orientation.

## Caution: School Zone

Sexual harassment is almost universally considered grounds for disciplinary action at school, at school-sponsored events, on the way to school, and on the way home from school.

## Sexual harassment includes but is not limited to the following:

1. Touching somebody's body on purpose in a sexual way (example: patting someone's rear); making unwelcome comments about somebody's physical sexual characteristics (either compliments or criticisms).

2. Making uncalled-for sexual remarks or propositions.

3. Accusing people of being gay or lesbian and/or hounding people who are gay or lesbian.

4. Flirting with someone who has indicated that they're not interested.

The rules apply to everyone: Both boys and girls are protected.

## In other words . . . Some of the Don'ts!

Hands off.

Don't touch, don't grope. Don't make fun of girls' (or boys') bodies. Don't make a big scene about what a babe somebody is. Don't whistle or catcall at people who pass by. Don't make random sexual remarks. Don't make wisecracks about how much you'd like to have sex with a certain other person. Don't tell sexual jokes to a person or audience you don't know well.

Permanently lose gay slurs. Omit the words *fag, faggot, dyke,* etc., from your vocabulary.

Avoid making verbal predictions about someone else's sexual orientation.

### HEADS UP!

An inherent human characteristic is that we long for connection, not separation. Not only is it against the rules to harass other people, it is also socially unacceptable, uncool, and will end up isolating you. Feel a need to harass and/or bully? See page 47. You may need help with an underlying problem.

## Don't tailgate!

If you have a romantic interest in another person who isn't interested, back off!

Following someone home, hanging out in front of somebody's house, calling over and over, sending unwanted gifts or flowers, making hang-up calls, repeatedly e-mailing and writing letters, waiting to catch glimpses of the person as they go about their daily life, or otherwise hounding another person may fall into the category of stalking, which is against the law.

## Is it okay to hold open a door for a girl?

Sure. If it seems like a polite thing to do, go for it—especially if she's carrying packages, walking with an older person, holding a baby, or leading kids through a doorway.

But use your head: If she's on your soccer team and you're heading through the door to the gym, she'd probably rather be treated like one of the guys.

Is it okay to offer to carry something heavy for a girl?

Sure, why not? But the operative word is *offer*.

"Want some help?" would be a good thing to say—rather than "Here, let me do that. You'll hurt yourself."

## SEXUAL ASSAULT

Since sexual contact requires both partners' consent, all forms of unconsented-to purposeful sexual touching are illegal.

## Oops!

What if you accidentally touch someone, like if you accidentally brush up against a girl's butt?

As long as it's not "accidentally on purpose," which we all know means intentionally, it's okay. It would be appropriate to say, "Sorry—it was an accident." And everything should be fine.

Girls (and boys), like women (and men), almost always know the difference between an accidental touch and an on-purpose one.

## Rape

Rape is forced sexual intercourse.

It is highly uncommon for a boy to be forcibly raped by a girl or woman, but guys can be forcibly raped (sodomized) by other males.

## Rape Crisis

Anyone who is raped should get medical attention immediately.

If a doctor can treat a victim right away, he or she may be able to help protect a victim from getting infected with certain sexually transmitted diseases (or from getting pregnant) from the assault. The medical facility can hook the victim up with psychological help and support.

Also, evidence can be collected to help convict the rapist.

If you are raped, tell your parent. Call the police, your doctor, the emergency room of the hospital, or the Child Help USA National Child Abuse Hot

Line (see page 134) or call a rape crisis hot line number in your area. (Call 411 or 0 and ask the operator or look in the front of the phone book or in the white pages under "rape crisis.")

## Statutory Rape

At age 18, anyone who is not developmentally delayed or disabled, boy or girl, is felt to be lawfully old enough to give valid consent to sex. (But other elements of consent still apply. See page 120.)

Statutory rape is when two people agree to have sexual intercourse, but one of the two people is legally considered *too old* (the laws may vary from state to state) to have sex with a person who is legally *too young* to consent to sex (the laws may vary from state to state). Complicated? It can be. Questions? Call Child Help USA (see page 134). Remember: The hot line's for teens, too.

## Date Rape

Otherwise known as "acquaintance rape," date rape is an assault that happens in the context of people getting to know each other romantically. Basically, what happens is that one person fails to honor the word "no" or other indications of "no" and forces the other into having sexual intercourse—often after they have been kissing, making out, or touching each other sexually.

Date rape is just as wrong and illegal as rape and statutory rape. All are serious criminal offenses—felonies, punishable by incarceration in jail or a juvenile facility.

Although acquaintance rape usually involves a guy assaulting a girl, it can also involve a guy assaulting another guy. It rarely, if ever, involves a girl raping a guy.

## Rape and Alcohol and/or Drugs

What if someone has sex with somebody who seems willing to have sex, yet is profoundly impaired by alcohol (or drugs)?

If intercourse occurs under the circumstances of one person being too drunk (or drugged) to give valid consent, the intercourse is considered "unconsented to" and, therefore, *rape*.

Having sexual intercourse with someone who is passed out (unconscious) or totally out of it as a result of having taken or been given drugs is rape.

# CHAPTER 14

# ROAD
## *Hazards:* KNOWING WHO AND WHAT TO AVOID

At some point during your journey, you're bound to run into roadblocks here and there. The best way to handle 'em is to get informed, trust your instincts, and do your best to avoid those types of situations. This chapter is intended to help you become aware of potential dangers and scenarios and to help you learn how to deal with them.

### *Perv Alert*

When my husband, Bob, was about 7 years old, he lived in a trailer park with his parents and big brother, Richard. Richard was much older than Bob. He was in his late teens and about to join the army.

One afternoon, a neighbor—a high school student that Bob had seen around the trailer park—invited Bob into his family's trailer to "show him something."

Nobody else was home when they went in.

The guy turned to Bob and said, "Let's take off our clothes." This seemed like a bad idea to Bob. But before he could even say no, the guy had unzipped his pants and stepped out of them, along with his underwear.

Bob didn't know anything about sex or kid molesters. He did know this much: It was pretty weird for some guy he hardly knew to suddenly be standing buck naked in front of him for no good reason.

So Bob charged back out of the guy's trailer and raced home.

"Did you tell your dad?" I asked him.

"No."

"Why?"

"I don't know."

"Did you tell your mom?"

"No!"

"Why not?"

"I told my big brother."

"What did he do?" I asked.

"I'm not sure. There was some kind of confrontation. After that, the kid and his family left the trailer park."

Some people think of a kid molester as a dirty old man—or a guy who looks like a sleazeball. But a child molester can be young or old, single or married, clean or dirty, male or female, rich or poor, gay, straight, or bisexual.

Some people think of a molester as a guy that

looks like he just crawled out from under a rock. But molesters can be distinguished-looking—some wear expensive suits and ties. They can be uniformed. They can be handsome and buff, and stylin'. They can be jocks.

Most people think of child molesters as adults or older teens, but even a kid can be a child molester if he or she forces sexual contact with another kid or has "agreed to" sexual contact with a significantly younger person.

**HEADS UP! Questions about "significant" age differences?** Call the Child Help USA National Child Abuse Hot Line (see page 134) to speak to a trained professional.

### We're not just talking about stranger danger.

Young children, preteens and teens, boys, girls, or both may become targeted by a molester.

Preadolescents and adolescents are often

targeted by older teens and adults, so stay on your toes!

Most molesters are known and trusted, and sometimes they're in a position of authority.

The molester is often a relative (see page 134).

A molester may be a teacher, coach, or religious leader. Often, molesters get jobs or work as volunteers in situations where they will have easy access to children.

Or they just choose careers that will put them in positions where they have an opportunity to get close to children.

Child molesters take advantage of younger people because they're smaller, less experienced, easier to confuse, and more vulnerable to attack—both physically and psychologically. But even a very small kid can have power against an older person who attempts abuse. The power lies in:

1. Trusting the feeling that something is wrong.
2. Saying no, getting away.
3. Reporting what happened, without delay.

### HEADS UP!

**The laws against child abuse are made to protect children and teens, including those who don't recognize that sex with a significantly older person is harmful.**

**The rules protect the victim even if he or she initiates and welcomes the contact. This is true even if the sexual contact felt good to the victim physically.**

**It's not the victim's fault!**

**Anyone who says something different is lying.**

➤ In addition to experiencing physical and emotional trauma, children who have sexual contact with adults are at risk for getting sexually transmitted diseases (see page 86). Girls can also become pregnant.

## BUILT-IN RADAR SYSTEM

### *Trust your instincts.*

Kids have an instinctive feeling that something is

wrong when an adult or significantly older person tries to start up sexual contact. It's very important to pay attention to these gut feelings. It seems wrong—because it is wrong.

If a situation is making you feel weird, pay attention to that feeling. Your inner voice tells the truth.

Listen when it tells you, "Something's happening that doesn't seem right. . . ."

Don't dismiss your instincts.

Instead, rely on them.

Say no, get away, tell a responsible adult what happened (see the Child Help USA National Child Abuse Hot Line info on page 134).

### *Know fear.*

If you feel "creeped out" by something somebody says or does, don't try to talk yourself out of it. Accept that you feel afraid. Respect the feeling of fear. Your senses are giving you information so that you can act to make yourself safe.

### *Hmmmm . . .*

Feel confused about something that's already happened—and not sure why?

Good communication with parents can help keep you safe. Most adults are protective of children—and are quick to identify inappropriate behavior patterns in others. If a person or situation makes you feel uncomfortable, uneasy, embarrassed, worried, sad, confused, or afraid, these feelings may be danger signals. **Talk to your parent about these feelings**, even if you don't know why you have them.

### *Protect yourself—stay in charge.*

You may have been taught that kids are supposed to be respectful of adults, but kids aren't supposed to be respectful to all adults. Be rude to an adult who tries to have sexual contact with you—even if the person is in a position of authority, like a religious figure, camp counselor, teacher, coach, or someone else that's trusted by the community.

## *"Get the hell away from me!"*

You don't have to be nice to anyone who's trying to take advantage of you sexually.

So don't be.

Get away from the person. Say no in whatever way you think will be most effective in getting him (or her) to leave you alone. Then immediately tell another adult what happened. Tell even if you are scared or embarrassed, even if you are afraid no one will believe you because you have no witnesses to back you up. And keep telling until someone really listens to what you are saying and takes it seriously.

Leave it up to a responsible adult to decide what to do about the situation. Your only job is to tell— then let the adults take over. Tell right away, without waiting or worrying about the consequences. If the abuse involves a parent, tell the other parent, a stepparent, or another adult relative (see page 134).

Or tell your doctor, your teacher, your principal, a nurse, or any other adult you choose—like your best friend's mom or dad, for example.

You can call the police or the county's child protective services number (see box on page 46).

You can also call the Child Help USA National Child Abuse Hot Line (see page 134).

## READING THE ROAD SIGNS

Perv behavior includes a wide range of activities.

Unless the person is in your similar age group, is unrelated to you, and has your consent, a person should NOT touch any part of your body or act in any way calculated to cause sexual arousal.

Kisses between kids and older friends and family members should be regular old garden-variety affectionate kisses, fast ones. Not sexy kisses! Not open-mouth kisses, not long kisses or French kisses— and not gentle, tender kisses on the neck, ears, shoulders, or private places of the body.

## *"No way!"*

Hugging someone or sitting on somebody's lap should never involve having an adult or significantly older person purposefully rub their genitals against your body.

What's up with that?!

Regular old snuggling in bed with your family and friends is fine. But an adult (or older teen) should not secretly creep into bed with you in the middle of the night and get weird under the covers.

Give 'em the boot! Then get right up and tell somebody what happened.

There's a wide range of perv behavior, and it doesn't always involve touching.

Exposing oneself (one's genitals); showing pornographic pictures (pictures of people having sex); and asking kids to pose for photographs naked, partly dressed, or in sexual positions are other examples of perv behaviors—and there are lots more.

How do you know if perv behavior is going on?

Almost always, you just know.

## *Trust*

Among other things, trust is when somebody who's vulnerable isn't afraid to believe in the goodness and honesty of another person.

Kids can become vulnerable because of their age, size, and ability to cope emotionally, and the limits of their experience in relation to those around them.

Believing in, and not being afraid of, an older person in charge is about trust.

Being molested by a trusted older person is one of the saddest, scariest, and most troublesome

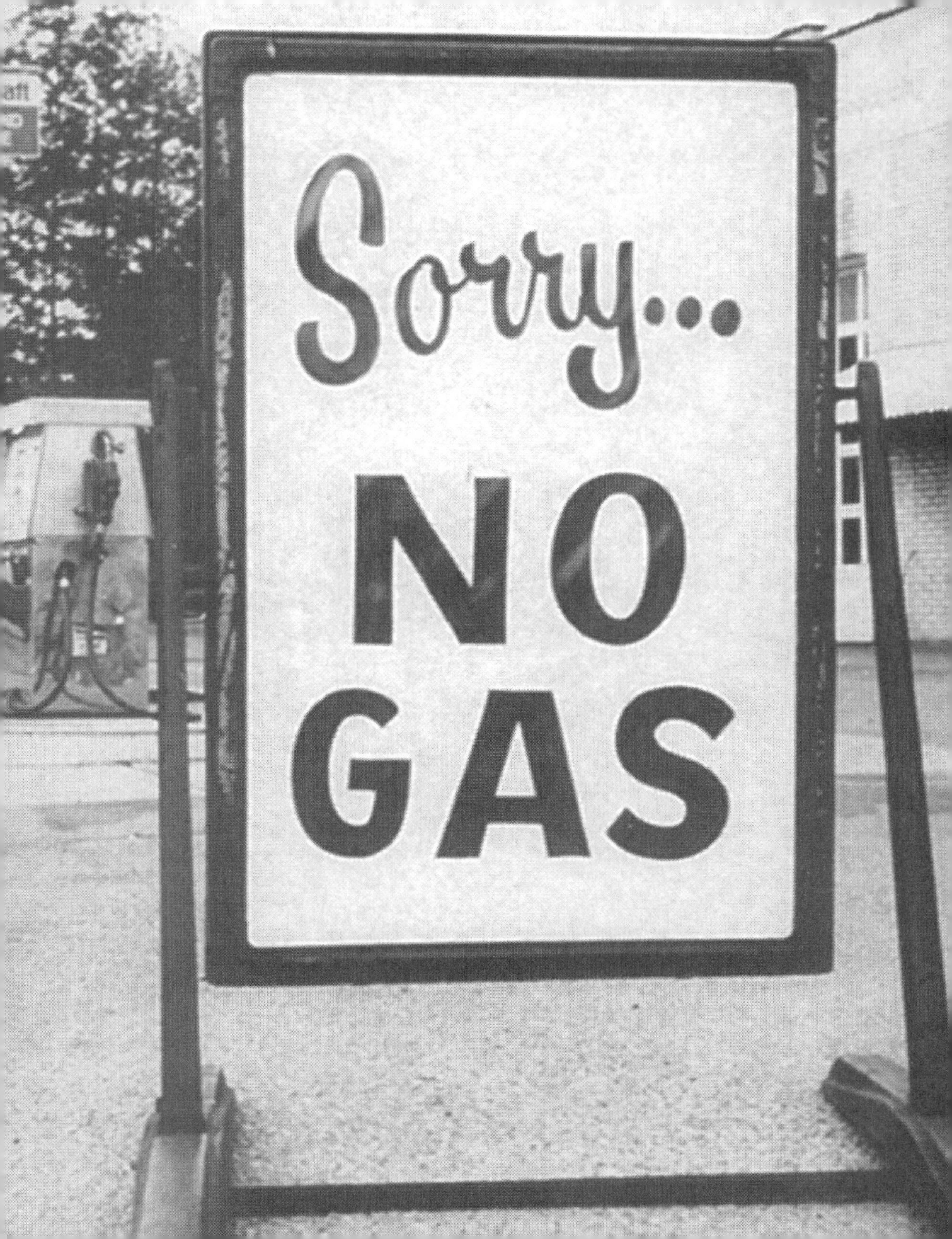
Sorry...
NO
GAS

things that can happen to a kid. It's just such a letdown! The betrayal of trust can be so huge, and the event can be so staggering, that you just can't make sense of it.

## A kid who's molested . . .

By a trusted older person or adult will typically feel embarrassed, ashamed, betrayed, humiliated, and afraid. And confused.

The molester gambles that because of these feelings, the kid won't want to tell anybody that he or she has been molested (or is being molested on a regular basis).

The molester also gambles on something else: that the victim will somehow feel responsible and blame himself. And the victim will be afraid that other people will blame him, too. But . . . the victim is never to blame!

## The victim is never responsible and never to blame.

Most sexual abuse of boys is perpetrated by adult (or teen) males.

Most kid/teen abusers are heterosexual (straight) males. Many are homosexual (gay) or bisexual males.

When boys are molested, it often involves their father, stepfather, grandfather, uncle, or older (or more powerful) brother, or another male family member or extended-family member, like a mother's live-in boyfriend (see page 134).

It's unusual for an adult woman to want to molest a preadolescent or adolescent boy—but it definitely does happen.

Some people call this situation "being seduced by an older woman." But it's really "being abused by an older woman."

That there's a female perpetrating abuse doesn't make it any less harmful to the kid.

Don't be flattered if an older woman seems interested in you sexually.

Stay away from her!

She's a perv!

And to top it off—she may have a sexually transmitted disease!

Get away from her and report her to your parent—or another trusted adult.

## HEADS UP!

Why would an adult or significantly older person propose that you do something together and keep it secret from your dad and/or mom? What might be proposed? Smoking cigarettes, smoking weed, drinking alcohol, looking at porn—or going to some forbidden place.

➤ **Ask yourself:**

What normal older person would rather secretly party, secretly look at X-rated pictures, or do other secret stuff with a young kid—than hang out with someone his (or her) own age?

An adult or significantly older person asking a kid to keep an activity secret is a signal that the person may want to separate a kid from the people most likely to protect him: his parents.

If this happens to you, what should you do? Say no. Then tell your parents about the conversation right away.

## Sometimes the molester makes threats.

Whether or not he or she will really carry out these threats depends on the situation; regardless, it's nothing anyone (especially not a kid) should try to guess at. The police need to be notified immediately. Kids and their family members become much safer once the police are notified that threats have been made.

The police, the people who work for kid protective services, and the counselors who answer the calls on the child abuse hot line can make immediate moves to rescue and protect children in dangerous situations (see the Child Help USA National Child Abuse Hot Line on page 134).

## Once a kid has been molested . . .

A complex set of psychological responses comes into play. If provided with a chance to recover from the trauma, he or she will probably end up being just fine. With the support of family, friends, and health care providers, kids bounce back.

But if the kid keeps the secret, there can be negative, lifelong consequences instead. He or she can become depressed (even suicidal). Shadowed by the secret, he or she may be unable to gain the confidence needed to live a happy, productive life.

And there are other troublesome possibilities. One is that a kid who's been molested and isn't given the opportunity to recover might go on to become a child molester in the future.

This is one of the reasons why patterns of child sexual abuse can repeat themselves for generations (see the Child Help USA National Child Abuse 24-Hour Hot Line on page 134).

## Help is just a phone call away.

If you or any kid or teen you know has a problem with being abused by anyone—including a relative—you can call the Child Help USA hot line number, the police, or your county's child protective services. (Dial 0 or 411 and ask the operator for the number. Or look in the phone book under "county government" listings under "social services," or in the white pages under "child protective services." Or call a youth crisis hot line [see page 46].)

If you need emergency help, call 911 or the police emergency number.

### ➤ Child Help USA National Child Abuse 24-Hour Hot Line (for Children, Teens, and Adults)

**This is the number:**
**1-800-4-A-CHILD (1-800-422-4453)**
**For the hearing-impaired:**
**1-800-2-A-CHILD (1-800-222-4453 [TTY])**

This hot line is set up to help with any kind of abuse, including sexual abuse, physical or emotional abuse, and neglect.

Anyone with questions or concerns about abuse can call it at any time of the day or night. It's free, and the call will not appear on the home phone bill.

If you call the hot line, you will get to talk to a trained professional. After you call, stay on the line. Keep waiting, and soon someone will answer and help you.

The purpose of the hot line is to help stop abuse. So, even someone who is afraid of abusing somebody else (or has) can call the hot line and get help.

## Incest—The Definition

The definition of incest may vary from place to place, but the following is a pretty universal guideline:

*Incest* refers to sexual relationships that take place between close family (or extended family) members:

parents and their offspring;
siblings;
close cousins;
aunts and nieces or nephews;

uncles and nieces or nephews;
grandparents and their grandchildren.

These sexual relationships are always against the law, even when the family members who are sexually involved with each other are consenting adults.

The unlawful relationships include people in a "step" or "half" relationship. They include people related through blood or marriage.

Innocent sexual experimentation between very young siblings of similar ages isn't considered particularly harmful—as long as it ends when kids are still very young.

Incest often involves children or teens being sexually abused within the family. Just like in the outside world, child molesting within a family is totally against the law. All of the rules are the same. Consent is never valid, even if the kid agrees to it. The molester gets in trouble when it's reported, not the molested person—and it's never, EVER considered the molested person's fault, no matter what.

This kind of sexual abuse within families involves an older or otherwise more powerful family member persuading, coercing, threatening, or somehow manipulating a younger or weaker or disabled kid in the family (or extended family) into tolerating or performing sexual acts, such as kissing, fondling, oral sex, anal sex, or intercourse.

When boys are molested within the family, it usually involves their father or stepfather. It also commonly involves a grandfather, uncle, or other stronger or older male member of the family or extended family—like a mother's live-in boyfriend.

But it is also possible for a boy to be molested by a *female* relative.

## Telling Versus Not Telling . . .
## No Contest: Tell.

Kids who are victims of incest usually don't want to tell because they think the family will be damaged if they do tell, and they're afraid that the relative who is abusing them will go to jail. Incest victims usually blame themselves. They feel guilty—even though it's not their fault. They don't want to talk about it.

Incest is one of the most frightening and upsetting situations imaginable for a kid. Some kids endure it silently—sometimes for years. But telling someone is the way to end the pain and confusion and start the healing process.

A family is already very damaged when a kid has suffered abuse by a relative. When abuse is reported, the family can be repaired. The kid can heal. The abuser is forced to confront his or her problems, often by participating in therapy or other programs.

Sometimes the abuser does go to jail, but not always.

In some cases, after the abuser gets treatment and counseling, it is possible for the family to be reunited under the supervision of the court— as long as the responsible adults in charge are convinced that the abuse won't happen again.

## When incest happens to a kid . . .

He or she may feel completely alone in the world, as if the situation has never occurred before. But the situation has occurred before, in many thousands of families.

Unfortunately, incest is common.

Since it's common, specially trained adults are able to help a kid and his or her family take steps to overcome the pain, fear, and confusion associated with it.

Counselors know how hard it is for a kid to ask for help in a situation involving incest.

## Friends don't let friends be abused.

Don't keep the secret if a friend (or family member) tells you about abuse. Kids who are being abused often tell other kids about abuse because they don't know where else to turn.

Even if you promise to keep the secret, don't. Get up your courage and tell a responsible adult.

You may feel like you'll be betraying the person who confided in you, but you won't be. You'll be asking a trusted adult for help on your friend's behalf. Ultimately, your friend (or family member) will understand that you did the right thing, the thing you were supposed to do under the circumstances. He or she will also understand that it was hard for you to break the confidence and that you did it because you cared.

# CHAPTER 15

# SAFETY
## *Zones:* STAYING SAFE AND IN CONTROL

Being alert, aware, and prepared to act helps keep you safe when you're out in the world alone (or with your friends).

Remember: Acquaintances, not just strangers, can pose a threat to a kid's safety. Think on your feet; stay in control of your situation. Don't give someone the opportunity to mess with you.

• Whenever possible, go places with a friend or family member rather than alone.

• Don't accept rides or enter vehicles without your parent's permission. Don't hitchhike.

• Don't take shortcuts alone through alleys, wooded areas, creek beds, railroad tracks, or other out-of-the-way places where you couldn't be seen or heard if you cried out for help. When you're alone, avoid parking lots and parking garages.

• If you become separated from your family, class, or group when traveling in an unfamiliar city, go to a pay phone and call 911 or dial 0 for the operator and ask to be connected to the police emergency number. Or ask someone who works in a store (wearing a name tag or working at a cash register) to call the police for you. Wait in as safe a place as possible. The police will

come and help reunite you with your group.

• If you go to a sporting event, concert, fair, or mall with your friends, decide in advance on a safe meeting place if you should get separated. Go there right away if you do get separated.

• If you're out with your friends and there's a change of plans, call your parent or one of the other kids' parent to discuss it. A responsible adult should know where you are and whom you are with.

• Unless there's a clear public safety emergency involving uniformed officers, or unless you need help from a uniformed officer, treat guys in uniforms as you would any other stranger. Uniforms are easy to rent or buy. If someone in a uniform approaches you with a concern or accusation, request that your parent be contacted. **Don't go anywhere** with him or her.

• Don't get an attitude or make personal remarks, comment on appearance, or say or do anything that might provoke a violent response from a kid not known to you. And don't respond violently if remarks are directed at you. Walk away. Kids out looking for a fight are usually dangerous—often armed. A kid with a problem

with violence can present a real danger to you, even if you're bigger. Back off; if you need help from an adult, get help.

• Don't allow adults you don't know well to engage you in conversations when you're out alone. You have no obligation to be polite or interact with adults who are strangers to you—so don't. When out alone, don't display your name visibly on your clothing, backpack, gym bag, or other belongings. It's easier for someone to trick you into talking to them if they know your name.

• Say no if someone you don't know well asks you to pose for a picture, video, or film; asks for your name, address, or school name; offers you a job or gift; offers you alcohol or drugs; or offers to show you pornography. Then tell your parent what happened.

**HEADS UP!**
Obviously, we need to be wary of strangers. But sometimes it's possible to find ourselves in a position where we have to reach out for help! If you urgently need help and there's no phone available, no law enforcement available, and no apparent safe place for you to go, you may need to ask someone you don't know to assist you. *If you have a choice, ask for help from a woman, a family, or an adult who has kids with him or her.*

## *Don't be lured away.*

Beware of an adult or older teen you don't know well who offers to show you something cool (like a motorcycle) and wants you to follow along alone to see it (like into a garage or house, for example). Responsible adults do *not* invite kids they don't know well and who are alone into houses, garages, or other isolated places.

If you discover that something of yours (like your bike or pack) has been moved close to a vehicle or place where someone could ambush you, leave it there. Don't walk up to it. Go get help from an adult.

## *If someone in a car pulls up to talk to you . . .*

Stand back and be ready to run. Cross the street or otherwise retreat to safety. Be suspicious of any adult or older teen who asks you for assistance or directions. Let the person get directions or assistance from someone his or her own age.

If you see a car circling the block or cruising your street, call the police and report it. Be ready to describe the car. It's fine to call anonymously (tell the police you don't want to give your name) if you want.

It would be very, *very* unlikely for someone to try to abduct you. But if grabbed by someone, fight your way free and make a lot of noise doing it. Cause the biggest scene you can so other people around can hear that you're in trouble and come to your aid.

Most adults will instinctively protect kids and teens in danger—but you need to get their attention first.

**FYI**
Some experts in law enforcement have the opinion that we should not agree to get into a vehicle with someone who's threatening us— even if they have a weapon. Those who have this opinion advise us to do the following:
1. Refuse to get into the vehicle, fight to get away, and make a lot of noise.
2. If pulled into a vehicle by an abductor and you can't get free, grab the wheel and cause an accident as soon as possible, while the vehicle is still moving relatively slowly. Act quickly! Turn the steering wheel into a parked car, sign, pole, or ditch (*not* into oncoming traffic or pedestrians).
Why?
There's no guarantee, but we're considered more likely to survive this type of low-speed accident than we are to survive being abducted and transported away in a vehicle.

*The National Center for Missing and Exploited Children (and Teens)*

There is a national center set up to help all missing, lost, abandoned, abducted, or runaway children. Every family and community wants missing children returned—no matter how far away they may be from home, no matter how long they've been gone, and no matter what has happened to them while they were gone. The National Center for Missing and Exploited Children (and Teens) hot line numbers are:

**1-800-843-5678 (U.S. and Canada)**
**For the hearing-impaired: 1-800-826-7653 (TTY)**

## *Home alone?*

When you answer the phone, don't give out information—get information. If someone asks, "Who's this?" answer with the question "Who's calling? Who do you want to speak to?"

Don't reveal that you are home alone. Say, "My dad (or mom) is unavailable to come to the phone right now. What's your number? I'll have him (or her) return the call."

Or use your answering machine to screen calls—picking up the receiver only when there is a familiar voice on the line.

Keep the doors locked. Don't open the door to anyone you don't know well. If someone hangs around after it's clear you're not going to open the door, call the police.

## *Sometimes people pretend there's an emergency to gain entry into a house.*

If a stranger comes to your door and says they need the phone to call the police, ambulance, or fire department, pick up your phone and call **911** (or the other police emergency number for your area). Tell the dispatcher there's someone outside the door needing to report an emergency. Ask that an

officer (and ambulance and/or fire truck, if that's what the person claims is needed) be sent over.

Then call through the door, "I've already called 911. The police are on the way here."

If there's an emergency, good, you've called 911. Now keep your door closed and locked until the police show up.

If there's not an emergency, even better that you called. You'll need the assistance of the police if somebody's trying to lie their way into your house. And good that you called through the door to say the police were coming. A person with bad intent would undoubtedly leave you alone once the police were on the way.

# TOURING ALONE ON THE INTERNET
## *Chat Rooms*

If you wouldn't interact with a stranger in a mall, why would you interact with a stranger on the Net?

The Internet is full of amazing, valuable information! It opens the door to so many interesting, exciting, and educational places.

But it can also open the door to weasels, sneaks, snakes, psychos, and pervs.

Make sure you don't "let them in." Have no expectation of privacy when on the Internet. Don't give out your name, address, phone number, school address, or parent's credit card information.

> ➤ **Chat Rooms**
> Adults posing as kids are continuously trying to get kids to interact with them on the Internet.
> The cute girl you imagine yourself to be chatting with could actually be some 45-year-old guy with a sex problem. Or a teen guy with a sex problem! Who cares how old he is! He's not who he's pretending to be!
> Talk on the phone? Exchange mail? Meet in person? Don't do it!

Chat rooms are perv paradise.

There have been lots of cases where pedophiles have used the Internet to trick or lure a kid into meeting—then raped, assaulted, and abducted the kid.

Or they've somehow weaseled information out of the kid and showed up at the kid's home or school.

If you do chat in a chat room, stay aware that you are communicating with an identity—a character—someone has created on a screen. There's a person behind this character.

Who is he or she, anyway?

### ➤ FILE A COMPLAINT

If someone proposes sex to you on the Internet, tell your parent. Your parent can report it to the Cyber-Tipline (www.cybertipline.com). This tipline is operated by the National Center for Missing and Exploited Children (see page 140).

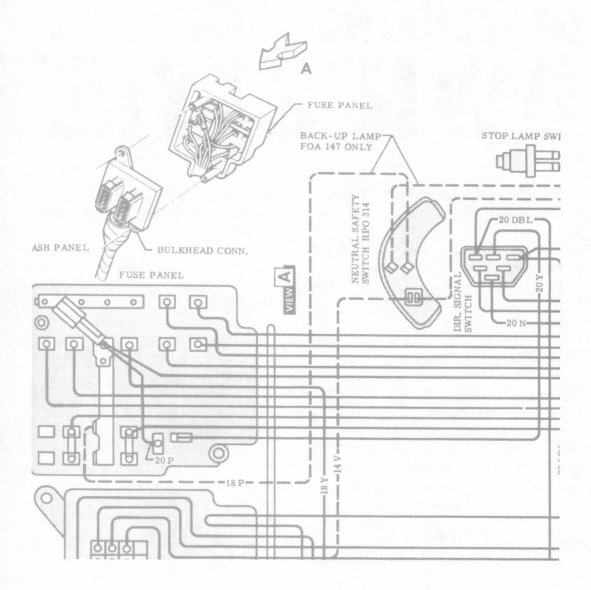

FUSE PANEL

BACK-UP LAMP
FOA 147 ONLY

STOP LAMP SWI

NEUTRAL SAFETY
SWITCH RPO 314

DIR. SIGNAL
SWITCH

20 DBL

20 Y

20 N

ASH PANEL

BULKHEAD CONN.

FUSE PANEL

VIEW A

20 P

18 P

18 Y

14 V

# CHAPTER 16

# Customizing:
# DEVELOPING YOUR
# OWN STYLE

## DEVELOPING PRESENCE AND STYLE

Developing a unique presence and sense of style doesn't happen overnight. It begins with the realization that appearance is more than just how a person looks and that style is more than appearance. Style involves attitude—beginning with your attitude toward yourself.

### Your Presence (Vibe)

Everybody has a vibe, a way of being in the world; be aware that things you say and do are making a statement about who you are.

### Your Style

You're born with certain looks, but you'll create your own style. You're about you. So don't measure yourself against other guys.

## UPHOLSTERY

No matter who you are, there will always be somebody with more expensive, more stylin', and just plain *more* clothes than you. It's possible to have a lot of style even if you don't have much money to spend on clothes.

### Shopping with a Parent

When you shop with your parent, you might run into some conflicts about what clothes you should wear. This is a normal part of growing up and establishing your identity.

The following suggestions may help you find some middle ground.

### Shopping Tips

1. After buying clothes, keep the tags on. Keep the bag and receipt until you have tried on the items at home. Try them on in front of the mirror. Like them? Still, wait until you're ready to roll: Wait till you've actually made the decision to wear each item before taking off the tags.

Keep the tags, receipt, and bag in your closet for a while—in case there's a flaw that doesn't show up until, say, after you wash or wear it a few

times. It's much easier to return clothing when you have the tags, bag, and receipt.

If you've bought something that has a defect, it's a very good idea to call the store and ask to talk to the manager. Explain the problem. Write down his or her name and find out when he or she works.

Return the merchandise when the manager is there—or ask the manager to make a note that you're coming in for a refund or exchange.

Since you've already discussed the problem, there shouldn't be a hassle when you show up.

2. Buy clothing loose enough to fit comfortably after being washed and dried a few times. Washing shrinks stuff, especially cotton. So does the dryer, even on "cool." Regarding pants and shorts: Is the waistband tight when you button or snap it? Do they ride up in the rear? If so, buy a bigger size—or you'll be miserable after they're washed and dried.

Jeans shrink in length over time, and you'll be getting taller. Pay close attention to the length of your pants—or they'll be floods after you wash them and put them in the dryer. Before you buy them, ask a salesperson how much you can expect them to shrink. If they shrink more than you were warned, bring 'em back!

Black pants, shorts, shirts, and jackets made of cotton (and denim) fade. You can hold off the fading process for a while by washing them inside out in cold water. Still, they won't remain as black as the day you bought them. And they'll keep on lightening over time. So ask yourself: Will I still like this if it's a couple of shades lighter? If not, don't buy it.

3. Read labels for washing instructions before buying. If it's dry-clean only—a shirt, for example—expect to spend about $5 or $6. Uh, each time you clean it? Yup. Avoid dry-clean-only clothes, unless they're for a really special event.

4. Unless you like to iron, think twice about buying clothes that require a lot of ironing to look good.

## Basic Threads

If you don't have someone to boss you around and pick out your clothes for you, here are some suggestions for a basic wardrobe.

## Dress Clothes

1. One pair of plain leather shoes, brown or black (these can easily be polished).

2. Two pairs of plain, dark, thinnish (not athletic) socks. Both pairs the same, in case the washing machine eats one sock.

3. A plain leather belt, with a plain buckle, that matches your shoes (brown or black).

4. One long-sleeved, collared cotton shirt (that can be bleached to rejuvenate it in case you get into a food fight wearing it).

5. One T-shirt to go under it.

6. One pair of cotton khakis, long enough to at least touch the tops of your shoes—but no so long that they eclipse the heels of your shoes in the back.

7. One tie—whatever one you like. Look in magazines for clues as to what's fashionable if you care.

8. One mid-weight dress jacket, sports jacket, or blazer—the most versatile would be a solid color. Navy, brown, or gray will work. Be positive the sleeves are long enough, since jackets are relatively expensive and your arms are growing—and will soon be dangling out of the cuffs. Better yet: Can you borrow a jacket? When you're growing fast, this may be the best option.

## Casual Clothes

1. Jeans. As mentioned previously, don't buy jeans that are threatening to be floods in the immediate future! Jeans shrink—a little or a lot, but always at least a little.

Is dark or light denim in style? Are flares, bells, or boot-cut, baggy, or slim-fit jeans in style? If you care, check this out in a magazine before shopping. (In the library, if you don't want to buy one.) Otherwise, just buy jeans you like that fit comfortably—not tightly.

2. A few colored T-shirts and/or other everyday shirts you like.

3. One solid-colored (goes with more things) warm sweater or sweatshirt—nice and big.

4. A jacket—if the climate calls for one. A hood is helpful.

5. One pair of flip-flops.

6. Pajamas—or at least one pair of pajama bottoms.

7. One pair of athletic shoes.

8. Some white athletic socks—all the same. That way, you won't have to match them; there will be endless possibilities for sock partnerships.

9. A few pairs of underwear.

**Seat Covers**
Boxers or Briefs?
Who cares!
Wear what's comfortable.

## Great Condition—Previously Owned

Wearing hand-me-downs from family or friends is one more way of recycling, being environmentally conscious, and being considerate of your parent's budget.

Any great "vintage" clothes available in the attic or way, way back in the family's closets? It's a fashion phenomenon: Styles that went out 20 years ago come back to haunt us.

Ask.

## GUY REPORT: BAD-HAIR LIFE

"In high school, I had hair from five different people's heads. It was curly in one spot, straight in another, frizzy somewhere else, thick here, thin there . . . etc. and all at once! Hair was very big in the high school I went to, so I was jittery and frustrated about it most of the time. I plastered it with Vitalis, Brylcreem, Tiger Balm . . . layers of grease or cut it all off almost like a skinhead and peroxided it white and wore a hat. Nothing worked. I remember looking in the mirror and thinking, If I just didn't have this hair and this skin (I had a vast array of acne as well), I might have a fighting chance.

"Fortunately, not long after that, the sixties came along, and I quit caring about hair pretty much forever from then on."

It's possible to put together a great look with hand-me-down clothes and clothes bought at garage sales, flea markets, and thrift stores. Artists, actors, models, musicians, and dancers (even movie stars) have been doing it for years.

Also, you can mix new stuff with used stuff; that's an old trick.

A tip if you shop in secondhand stores or flea markets: Plan to wash before you wear. Always give armpits a "sniff test." If the underarm doesn't smell good, don't buy it unless you're sure it's washable in **hot water and detergent**. (Buying a stinky used leather jacket is an example of what would be a bad choice; leather isn't washable, and dry-cleaning it would be really expensive.)

## HOW TO TIE A TIE

1. Situate the tie so that the end **A** is longer than end **B** and cross **A** over **B**.

2. Turn **A** back underneath **B**.

3. Continue by bringing **A** back over in front of **B** again.

4. Pull **A** up and through the loop around your neck.

5. Hold the front of the knot loosely with your index finger and bring **A** down through front loop.

6. Remove finger and tighten knot snugly to collar by holding **B** and sliding knot.

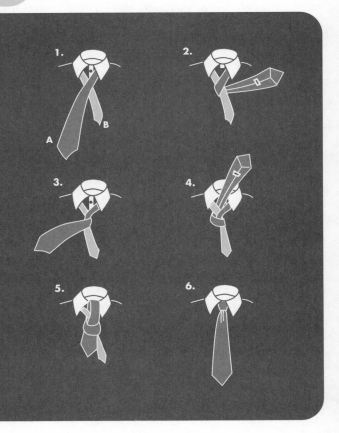

## ► Keep the ~~Cycle~~ Recycle Going

If you have clothes that you've grown out of or are sick of and they're still in good shape, get into the habit of stuffing them into a bag (an old pillowcase works) in your closet. Eventually the bag will fill up.

Then donate the clothes to a charitable organization—like your younger brother.

# ROOFTOPS
## *Hairstyles*

Hair grows naturally in a variety of colors and textures. All hair can look good in its natural state. Just keep your hair clean and trim it occasionally. It will look and smell great.

There are lots of hair products available for guys. They can make your hair shine, stick straight up, or lie down flat. They're commonly sold in drugstores. If you're curious, check them out.

Note conditioners (displayed near shampoos). They can be rinsed out or left in after washing, and they increase manageability.

You can stand up against frizz, too—with a little help from the products developed to tangle with it.

And speaking of tangling, detanglers can help you untangle long hair.

Interested in alternative hairstyles? Lots of kids are, especially kids who are artists or musicians and appreciate a more unconventional look.

As long as you have your parent's okay, and as long as your school's dress code allows for it, there's no reason not to experiment.

Use products responsibly.

There are countless products that alter the natural state of hair. *Always ask* permission of your parent before using these.

Read the warning label on the package carefully before you buy any of these products. Most products such as relaxers, perms, bleaches, and dyes require adult supervision. Why? They can damage your eyes. Study the warnings on the packaging and follow all directions, paying close attention to the protection of your eyes.

Don't *ever* bleach or dye your eyebrows or eyelashes.

## HEADS UP!

If you accidentally get a potentially damaging hair product in your eyes, *immediately* begin flushing your eyes with water.

Catch a gentle stream from the faucet in your hand and blink into it, or use an eye cup, or ask a helper to pour water gently into your eye from a clean cup or pitcher while you tip your head back. Forget about getting wet. You can change your clothes later.

*Continue flushing your eyes for 15 minutes—* then call a doctor or poison control center number for additional advice. The poison control number for your region will probably be listed on the emergency page in the front of the phone book. Or call the information operator for the number.

## *Moon Roof*

In some parts of the United States, a shaved head is considered an emblem of extremist viewpoints linked with ignorance, racism, hatred, and violence.

In other areas, having a shaved head is just another hairstyle.

Make sure you know what's up if you're contemplating shaving your dome. And do ask your parent's permission.

A helper is usually required to do a good job and/or to avoid totally nicking up your scalp.

Remember not to share safety razors. It is possible (although improbable) for somebody else's blood to be on the blade; blood carries germs, including HIV (see page 89).

## *Door Dings*

During adolescence there's a tendency to focus on very small physical imperfections and stress over them, as though physical perfection actually exists.

Which it doesn't. Guess what—you're not perfect. You're not supposed to be! And the really good news is that neither is anybody else.

Bumps, moles, warts, flaky skin, cowlicks, hairy nostrils, and pointy heads aren't factory defects. They're just small variations in human design.

## GUY REPORT: ERASERHEAD

"When I was in grade school and the weather was bad, we played games in the classroom instead of going outside to recess. One of the games was an 'eraser relay.' Two groups of kids could get at each end of the room and race down the aisles between our stupid little desks trying to balance black chalkboard erasers on our heads while moving as fast as we could to transfer it to the next kid's head.

"This was the time of the early flat-tops, so most of the boys could accomplish the feat with ease. My own case, however, was different. Because my mother had a terrible time during my birth, I was extricated into this world by large forceps . . . pliers. The result was my having a very pointed head.

"Instead of a flat top, I had a roof top. I had to lay my head cheek-to-shoulder to get the proper flat angle to carry the eraser.

"I always dreaded this foul-weather game because I could not do it well and it pointed out my awful physical oddity."

### Be real.

People come in all shapes and shades and sizes. Appreciate your unique characteristics.

You don't have to look like a model or a movie star to be handsome.

You don't have to be handsome to be beautiful. You don't have to be buff to be powerful.

You don't have to be big to be strong.

And besides, you don't have to be strong—not all of the time, anyway.

Who you are is defined by what you do, say, and think. It's defined by how you act and who you are, not how you look. What's in your head and what's in your heart are the most important things. In the long run, success is less about appearance—and more about performance using life skills that you've developed like integrity, courage, and compassion.

### Low Mileage

You're a kid. Pubic hair and ejaculations don't change that. Looking physically like an adult male doesn't mean you're supposed to take on the roles and responsibilities of a man. You're a kid—entitled to the care and protection of the adults around you.

Life isn't a race. So take it slow and easy. You're not supposed to know exactly where you're going or where you'll end up.

The journey is the destination.

### An Insurance Policy

Communicate with your family and friends—especially about things that trouble you. Talk! It'll help keep you covered, bumper to bumper.

### Keep your lifetime warranty in effect.

Wear your seat belt. Wear your helmet!

Don't do drugs. Don't let anybody who's drunk or stoned drive you anywhere.

Postpone having sex with a partner until you are fully mature and able to accept the risks and responsibilities.

Look for non-violent solutions to conflict.

Maintain realistic expectations of yourself and the people around you.

Think for yourself; don't give into the feeling that you have to do what other kids are doing to belong. You belong!

Accept yourself. Hear your own ideas and pay attention to your own instincts about what is right, or wrong, for you.

Work hard.

Play hard.

Make plans.

Dream.

# INDEX

EAST SMITHFIELD PUBLIC LIBRARY

3 2895 00085 6174